# SEE ME

Developing self-confidence and an assertive approach
for ordinary people in everyday situations at work
(and at play!)

## Joanna Gutmann

See Me

Published by Blue Ocean Publishing
St John's Innovation Centre
Cambridge CB4 0WS
United Kingdom

www.blueoceanpublishing.biz

Typesetting by Norman Brownsword, Spitfire Design

A catalogue record for this book is available from the British Library.

ISBN 978-0-9556430-9-5.

# Contents

# Introduction

## Why 'See me'?

The book got its title from a course delegate, who said, 'They see only an extension of the keyboard, or maybe a person to give work to, but they don't see me ... the human bending under the pressure, invisible in meetings and finding ever more work piling up.' Her problem was twofold: the need to increase her assertive skills in dealing with specific situations and the need to generally have a greater presence in the office – to be noticed or seen.

So *See me* sets out to provide help for anyone in such a position. It is a self-help book which combines development of assertive skills and communication with guidance on creating a more professional, competent impression. Along the way, your self-esteem and self-confidence will benefit.

## Self-confidence

Self-confidence is, as it sounds, having confidence in your ability, power and judgement; being happy with yourself and comfortable in your own skin.

Assertiveness and self-confidence are closely linked in that if you are confident within yourself, you will naturally behave more assertively.

Look at Hannah's response to a question when among friends.

*Amy:      We should get going, the film starts in a couple of hours ... where shall we go for some food?   The steakhouse?*

*Hannah:   I'm veggie!   There's a new Italian up by the canal – I had a look at the menu and it's not expensive ... how about trying that?*

And when among colleagues in the team she joined three weeks ago:

*Alex:*    *First team outing of the year ... where shall we go for some food?*

*Hannah:*   *I don't mind.*

When Hannah was naturally confident, she had no trouble asserting herself; when not so sure of the people she was with, she didn't say anything about being vegetarian.

If you have confidence in yourself, you will be calmer, more positive and happier. You will communicate more clearly, which will make you more effective, and others will have confidence in you.

## Self-esteem

Your self-esteem is, as it sounds, the esteem in which you hold yourself. If you don't believe, in yourself, you are going to find it hard to be seen as self-confident and assertive. If your self-esteem is good, you will find it easier to be honest and clear in your dealings with others, and less afraid of potential problems and setbacks. If your self-esteem is low, every setback is further proof of your low worth.

### How's your self-esteem?

| | | |
|---|---|---|
| I look in the mirror and I see | my physical 'faults' | my attributes and/or the whole picture |
| I remember from my past | uncomfortable or difficult situations | a selection of things depending on circumstance |
| I make a mistake and | lie awake at night thinking about it | deal with it and try to move on |
| If someone's view is different to mine | I tend to change my view to match | It's interesting to discuss the differences |
| If I try something new | I expect it to go wrong | I hope it will go well |
| If it's difficult | I give up easily | I look for ways to manage |

Look at your answers, then choose:

I have                    poor self-esteem         good self-esteem

**Building self-esteem**

It's not a particularly easy task. If your self-esteem is low, you are likely to have many years of negativity and uncomfortable past experiences to overcome. But you've made a start in reading, or at least buying, this book, so it's worth carrying on.

### What's the problem?

Sit down quietly and identify what it is that's lowered your self-esteem. Were you bullied at school? Have you failed to achieve desired targets? Were you compared unfavourably to your siblings? Abandoned by an adored partner? Be honest with yourself; no one else needs to know your thoughts.

### Start to redress the balance

Force yourself to identify your strengths, your talents, the positive aspects of your personality and life.

### Look the part

A large part of the communication process is non-verbal. Presenting yourself as confident, appropriately dressed and presented and projecting a calm, controlled presence will have a massive impact on how others see you. And if they see you as confident, they will treat you as confident, which will have a significant impact on your confidence.

Throughout this book, you'll find tips and advice for building your self-esteem and confidence.

## Assertiveness

Have you ever felt invisible? You feel invisible when your manager doesn't hear your point, colleagues don't notice you until they want you to do something, your partner doesn't realise that you need help, or the waiter doesn't catch your eye. Have you noticed that when you say you can't take something on, you end up doing it anyway? You have? Then you will probably be aware of the need for assertiveness.

Assertiveness is a behaviour style which involves recognition of self and others, clear communication and the confidence to make your case, whilst recognising that others might want something different.

'Assertive' is not a description of a person, it simply describes how they are behaving at a particular time. It is closely linked to your self-confidence and it is easier to be assertive when you are comfortable; for example, with a partner or friends. However, it is not so easy when you are not feeling comfortable with a person or in a particular situation, perhaps with senior management or with someone who has put you down before.

The good news is that, whilst it is easy to be assertive when you feel comfortable, it is quite possible to behave assertively when you do not. In other words, if you can't make it, fake it! This approach will change the way others perceive you and thus how they react to you – if they see you 'behaving' competently and confidently, they are more likely to treat you as competent and confident. This, in turn, boosts your self-esteem and self-confidence, which helps improve your communication still further.

Communicating assertively doesn't mean that you 'win', but it certainly increases your chances of coming away equal. We often fail to get what we want because we simply don't make ourselves clear. Consider the example below:

Claire:    Please would you collate the complaints figures this week; the board meeting is on Monday.

Jess:    It's difficult this week, I've been so busy with this report and the end-of-year stuff is taking most of my time.

Claire:    Well, I'll leave them with you anyway.

Jess thought she'd said she was too busy to do the figures this week, Claire thought that although Jess was busy, the job would get done. On Friday, when it's clear the figures won't be collated for the board meeting, Claire will feel let down, particularly since (she 'knows') Jess said she would be able to do it. Jess will be resentful of Claire's anger because she's said she couldn't do it. Alternatively, Jess will end up working late, angry with Claire for ignoring her and with herself for not standing up for herself.

## Why be assertive?

Quite simply, for an easier life. Assertive communication is simpler, clearer and encourages you to take responsibility for yourself and think positively. In difficult situations, it will help you to be realistic and work constructively towards an acceptable outcome.

Developing self-confidence and assertive behaviour are not difficult, but do take a bit of time and effort. People start from different positions and some will always find it easier than others and develop their skills faster.

This book will help you build your self-confidence and develop your assertiveness. You will be guided through making small changes immediately and building your skill over the next few weeks.

### And until you can make it, fake it!

A lot of your self-confidence comes from how others treat you. If you show a lack of self-confidence, people won't have faith in you and will treat you accordingly ... which leads to a drop in your self-confidence. It's important to behave as the person you'd like to be, not as the person you feel you are; so, as you read through the book, think how you can demonstrate confidence, even if you don't feel confident.

*Jenny felt intimidated in the company of senior management and was almost relieved that the three directors on her floor didn't seem to notice her. She was a bit ashamed and didn't like the feeling, describing herself as 'pathetic'. Her colleague pointed out that she almost always looked at the floor as she walked, so she made a great effort to look up and engage brief eye contact with those she passed. Although she still felt uncomfortable, no one seemed to notice this, and she soon found people saying 'good morning' or 'hello' as she passed. Accordingly, her confidence grew, and she was delighted to hear herself commenting on the hot weather as she travelled in the lift with a senior manager.*

# Using the book

The book is structured in three parts. The first explains the different behaviours in the context of assertiveness and the rights on which they are based. The second looks at creating a general image of confidence and competence. The third focuses on different situations and how you can create the right impression for each.

It is a workbook; the sections are short, so you can work through it or dip in and out, choosing the parts which are particularly relevant to you. Whatever section you are working on, work through it, consider its relevance to your behaviour, identify changes you want to make and then go and practise them. Use the 'See me' sections to guide you and help you plan for changes to your approach or behaviour in the future.

Throughout the book there is advice, there are tips and there is general guidance with case studies to help you identify with situations and behaviours. Throughout, there is the dual aim of genuinely building your self-esteem and confidence, as well as perfecting the art of creating the right impression.

You are unlikely to learn without suffering some setbacks on the way. You might be misunderstood, lose confidence and back out before taking your planned action, or sink back into passive behaviour. That is no problem; in fact it's normal! When it happens to you, sort out what went right and where the problem occurred. Decide why it happened.

*Max* *wanted to approach his team leader, Steve, about the backing track that was being used on an advert his team were creating. He knew from past experience that Steve was not particularly open to suggestions and tended to react as though his professionalism was being challenged. Max went to see Steve, but part way through his explanation he could see it was going nowhere and backed down. Over a beer with his brother that evening, he explained and realised it went wrong when Steve leaned back, put his hands behind his head, sighed with boredom and 'looked down his nose' at Max.*

*Max spent a couple of days running through what he wanted to say, and prepared himself for the typical response before returning to Steve's office. Steve exhibited the same behaviour, but this time Max carried on, making sure that he behaved as though Steve was showing signs of real interest. They ended up discussing the track and, although Max didn't get all the changes he wanted, his views were taken into account and some were incorporated into the final advert.*

## Small steps

There is nothing wrong in having a grand action plan for significant changes, but do not underestimate the importance of small successes. Every time you walk through the office with your head high, you are adding a small step on your ladder to success. Each time you say just a couple of words of agreement in a meeting, you are 'being seen' and working towards a larger, more confident contribution.

*Good luck!*

# 1 Passive behaviour

*No one hugs a doormat ...*
*... in fact, most people don't even notice the doormat;*
*they just walk over it ...*
*... wiping their feet on it as they go!*

How often have you found yourself helping a colleague when you don't have the time to spare, or not liking to say that you don't understand an instruction, or watching a film you do not want to see?

You are behaving passively when:

your manner is apologetic, so your message loses its impact

*'I know I haven't worked here long, but ...'*
*'I'm not very experienced, but ...'*

you put yourself down

*'I'm only the receptionist.'*
*'You know me – can't add up to save my life.'*

you keep quiet

*'I don't mind.'* (when you do)

you agree to do something without saying you had other plans/pressures.

This type of behaviour is damaging because it wears you down. If you keep telling yourself that you are useless, you will come to believe it. Equally importantly, if you keep sending small messages highlighting incompetence, other people will come to see you as incompetent. Consider the short examples below and think what sort of impression is created if Daniel keeps sending this type of message.

*Amanda:*  *How did you get on with that report?*

*Daniel:*  *It's on your desk, but I'm not sure whether it will be any good.*

Or

*Amanda:*   *Have you got hold of the engineer yet?*

*Daniel:*    *Oh, I'm sorry – I did try this morning and left a message, but I haven't heard from him.*

Daniel's report may, or may not be, good, but there's no point in sowing the seeds of doubt in his manager's mind. In the second example, he has the task under control, but gives the impression that he has not.

Better responses would be, 'It's on your desk' and 'I left a message this morning and will ring again after lunch if I haven't heard by then'.

Another common example of passive behaviour is saying yes instead of the no you want to say. As a result, you end up taking on extra work, staying late, covering school runs and helping with jumble sales. There's a whole section devoted to this later in the book.

# Why do people behave passively?

There are many reasons, but some of the most common are that they:

- feel uncomfortable with someone they perceive as 'more important' because of their job or position

- have had an earlier row or bad experience with a person

- have had a bad experience of what they perceive as that 'type' of person

- are just having a 'down' day

- are in a general spiral of negativity and poor self-image

- have allowed passivity to become their default behaviour.

### How do you know you're behaving passively?

❑ You keep quiet when you want to speak.

❑ You say yes when you want to say no.

❑ You try to say no, but use words like 'maybe', 'possibly', 'it's difficult' instead.

❏ You say sorry when you haven't done anything wrong.

❏ You put yourself down.

❏ You blame others instead of taking responsibility for yourself (*e.g. I would be happy to help, but Colin doesn't like it if I go out in the evenings*).

Others might see you as passive because:

❏ You don't make good eye contact.

❏ Your voice tone is giggly, hesitant or whining.

❏ You tend to bite your lip and/or have an unfocused giggly grin.

❏ Your posture is defensive, folded in.

❏ You shrug as though giving in.

❏ You don't take up much space.

❏ You think, 'They don't see me!'

## What is the effect on me?

You may feel short-term relief at having avoided an argument or an awkward situation. However, this is replaced by irritation with others for taking advantage of you – and at yourself for letting them.

You will take on too much because of an inability to say no. This will mean you get pressured and stressed, possibly feeling that you can't cope.

Behaving passively results in a general loss of self-confidence, a feeling of negativity and of being in the control of others. This causes stress in itself, even before the additional problems caused by taking on more than you can cope with.

## What's the effect on the other person?

Although we generally behave passively to please others and avoid argument, the effect is often the opposite. People are frustrated by your unwillingness to speak up, or by the barbed or sarcastic comments you might make out of frustration.

Consider the situations below:

**Sanjay** asked his colleague, Amy, if she could take an early lunch because he wants to meet a friend who is only available after 1.00pm. Amy agrees, but Sanjay finds out later that she had to cancel meeting her sister. Sanjay may feel guilty, but is equally likely to be irritated that Amy didn't say anything about her plans.

**Sue** is taking minutes and is completely baffled by some acronyms that are used. However, given the seniority of the participants, she keeps quiet and vows to ask her manager the next day. As a result, she misunderstands a substantial part of the discussion. When she later asks her manager for an explanation, the response is an exasperated, 'Why didn't you say at the time?'

**Tony** is not comfortable speaking in front of a large group of people, so keeps quiet in a meeting, even though he can see that the new staff rota will not suit his team. He is then left with the uncomfortable task of explaining an unpopular rota to his staff that he struggles to justify. They just see him as weak.

# What is the effect on a situation?

Because communication is not clear, misunderstandings occur and outcomes are agreed that are not practical or satisfactory. Issues need to be revisited and time is wasted with over-long communication.

Read the  points and questions below, then consider the case study before responding to them.

- Identify a situation, person or type of person that makes you behave passively.

- What is it about the person or their behaviour that causes you to behave in this way?

- How do you demonstrate the behaviour?

- What are the short-term effects of your behaviour on your mood or feelings?
- What are the longer-term effects?
- What are the outcomes?

**Cara** *is a newly-qualified social worker. She attends monthly departmental meetings, but tends to contribute little, even though she has lots of ideas. Sometimes she doesn't understand a point that's made, but is unwilling to say so.*

*Identify a situation, person or type of person that makes you behave passively.*

*The departmental meeting*

*What is it about the situation or behaviour that causes you to behave this way?*

*I'm conscious that they are all really experienced. I'm worried that I'll look stupid if I don't understand.*

*How do you demonstrate the behaviour?*

*I look down a lot. My manager teases me for 'peeping' under my fringe. I keep quiet.*

*How do you feel, short term?*

*Initially, relief that the meeting is over. Then frustrated that I didn't contribute, annoyed that someone who said something I'd been thinking was praised.*

*And long term?*

*I dread the meetings. I now feel I can't contribute. A bit guilty at not raising points that are relevant.*

*The outcomes:*

*My ideas are not raised and they might be good! New thinking isn't being brought into the meeting.*

## Now do it for yourself

• Identify a situation, person or type of person that makes you behave passively.

_____

• What is it about the person or behaviour that causes you to behave this way?

_____

• How do you demonstrate the behaviour?

_____

• What are the short-term effects of your behaviour on your mood or feelings?

_____

• What are the longer-term effects?

_____

• What are the outcomes?

_____

*At her supervision, **Cara** devised a four-stage plan with her manager to help build her confidence, deciding that she would:*

1. *Actively join in the conversation before the meeting started.*

2. *Sit centrally, engage eye contact and make sure she appeared involved, even if not actually speaking.*

3. *Agree verbally with something said in the meeting.*

4. *Ask a simple question for information or explanation.*

*Cara reinforced this over a couple of meetings and was soon more comfortable to participate.*

Define a staged plan to help you behave more assertively
in your chosen situation.

_____

_____

_____

_____

_____

## Catch a problem before it becomes an issue

It is much easier to deal with small problems than have to make a major
change to your behaviour. So, next time you catch yourself behaving
passively, just stop and think:

1. What did you do/say?

_____

2. What was the result of your passivity?

_____

3. What should you have done/said?

_____

Now practise saying it aloud (so it sounds natural to you); close your
eyes and visualise the encounter with the outcome you wanted.

Next time, be alert to the situation and try to catch yourself before you
give in.

## And finally

Identify three general changes you could make to the way you look,
move or speak to help yourself be seen as less passive:

1. _____

2. _____

3. _____

# 2 Aggressive behaviour

*Very few people are out to get you ...*
*... most who behave aggressively are just so focused on where they're going that they don't notice you.*

Consider these three speech therapists:

**Mandy** could be called a bully – she's sarcastic, short-tempered and quick to blame anyone other than herself when things go wrong. She regularly points out the failings of her colleagues and managers, both directly to them and behind their backs.

**Sam** is highly energetic; he's always looking for the next project and enthusiastically throws himself into everything, always full of ideas.

**Elvi** is stressed; her caseload is more than she can handle. She's behind with the admin, is working late and taking work home. She's finding it difficult to concentrate and is sleeping badly.

**Verbal violence**

Ask someone to describe aggressive behaviour and they will typically describe a character like Mandy. This form of aggressive behaviour involves sarcasm, put-downs, shouting, pointing, and so on. This constant dismissal of others reinforces her positive view of her own 'rightness'. She often justifies her behaviour by feeling that 'they deserved it' and her communication style does achieve short-term results.

However, this type of aggression tends to keep the body in ongoing readiness for 'attack', which is physically and mentally draining. Those on the receiving end of the aggression tend to withdraw, at best complaining when out of earshot or, eventually, actively working against the aggressor. This reinforces the idea that others are incapable or 'out to get me' and confirms the need to be aggressive.

## Tunnel vision

But aggressive behaviour is simply putting yourself before others, and in the workplace there are many more like Sam and Elvi – people who are so caught up in their own work that they don't register others. As costs are cut, there are fewer people to do the work and the pressure builds. As a result, orders are given instead of requests made; everyday courtesies are forgotten.

Sam and Elvi have very different causes for their aggressive behaviour. Sam is simply so enthusiastic about the latest project that he assumes everyone else feels the same and is with him. As a result, he doesn't ask for help – he assumes it:

Sam:     *Elvi, I'm glad I've caught you. If this office move is to be a success, we have to draw up a really detailed spreadsheet, so everyone can chart what is going where in the new building. Since you are undoubtedly the spreadsheet queen, I've left it on your desk – it will need to be done before the meeting tomorrow afternoon. Must dash, I've got to see Martin.*

Although the reason for Elvi's aggressive behaviour is different, the effect is the same:

Elvi:    *Oh Tom, I'm glad I've caught you. Sam's a nightmare – he's given me this spreadsheet to do. It's not difficult, but I just don't have the time to do it – I've got all these reports to do and they have to be in before lunch on Monday and now I've been asked to cover a clinic this afternoon and see a new patient on my way home. If I leave it on your desk ... oh there's my phone – thanks.*

Sam, in his enthusiasm, just assumed Elvi would do the task and she, overworked and stressed, did the same to Tom.

Most people, particularly those who buy a book like this, don't like to think of themselves as behaving aggressively, but it's a rare person who doesn't sometimes do it! For example:

- when tiredness or frustration makes you snappy:

    *Give it here, I'll do it ... it's only a computer.*

- when we ask for help without checking whether the other person is able/willing to do so:

  *Can you collect the children at five?* (without waiting for an answer)

- when you make a decision for the group without consultation:

  *Come on, let's go to that new pizza place.*

Note that in the last two, it is the lack of giving the others the chance to respond that makes it aggressive behaviour.

## What is the effect on me?

There is usually a short-term reward for aggressive behaviour – it does get things done. You might feel relief at having 'sorted it', but the negative physical effects of the body remaining in attack mode are likely to culminate in problems.

## What is the effect on the other person?

Although you might get things done, the overall result is almost guaranteed to be negative. Verbal violence causes hurt and upset and sometimes results in a similar response. Even aggression caused by tunnel vision upsets people, as they often feel put-upon and taken for granted.

## What is the effect on the situation?

The outcome can be an argument if the other person 'fights back', but commonly people don't say anything directly. Instead they go underground, talking behind your back, sometimes scheming against you. Although they may do what you ask, it is seldom to the best of their ability and they are unlikely to give their own ideas and suggestions.

## How do you know you're behaving aggressively?

❏ You get snappy when you're tired.

❏ You tend to be sarcastic.

❏ You make decisions when the others are faffing around.

❏ While they dither, you act.

❏ You assume they want what you want.

❏ You use emphatic words like 'must', 'vital', 'essential'.

Others might see you as aggressive because:

❏ you get really enthusiastic about things

❏ you talk a lot

❏ you are surprised when others are not as keen on something as you are

❏ you can be sarcastic

❏ you stare people down

❏ the muscles in your face get tense

❏ you take up a lot of space (in relation to your physical size)

❏ you tend to 'tut' or sigh.

Read the points and questions below, then consider the case study before responding to them.

• Identify a situation, person or type of person that makes you behave aggressively.

• What is it about the person or behaviour that causes you to behave this way?

• How do you demonstrate the behaviour?

• What are the short-term effects of your behaviour on your mood or feelings?

• What are the longer-term effects?

- What are the outcomes?

**Antonia** *is a senior social worker and team leader. She attends monthly departmental meetings, but she views them as a waste of time – they are badly chaired and last longer than they should. She often keeps quiet, looking at her watch and hoping that her vibes will be picked up by the chairperson. However, some of her colleagues say some really stupid things and often go over the same ground again and again; she feels she has to say something, so they can get through the business and back to the proper job.*

Identify a situation, person or type of person that makes you behave aggressively.

*The departmental meeting.*

What is it about the person or behaviour that causes you to behave this way?

*Frustration at so much time taken, but so little achieved. They just gossip.*

How do you demonstrate the behaviour?

*I look at my watch a lot. I tut and put my pen down. I tend to sit back and stare into middle distance, probably with my arms folded.*

How do you feel short term?

*I can feel the frustration building.*

And long term?

*I'll probably just stop going to the meetings and wait for the minutes.*

The outcomes

*I won't be 'in the loop'; others might think I don't care.*

- Identify a situation, person or type of person that makes you behave aggressively.

- What is it about the person or behaviour that causes you to behave this way?

  _____

- How do you demonstrate the behaviour?

  _____

- What are the short-term effects of your behaviour on your mood or feelings?

  _____

- What are the longer-term effects?

  _____

- What are the outcomes?

  _____

*After following this process, **Antonia** decided she would:*

- *explain to the chairperson that it wasn't possible for her to give a full hour to the meetings*

- *ask if time could be saved if there was an agenda for the meetings*

- *pass some handouts from a 'managing meetings' course to the chairperson*

- *accept that some of her colleagues only met at these meetings and they needed the opportunity to chat.*

*Define a staged plan to help you behave more assertively in your chosen situation:*

### Catch a problem before it becomes an issue

It is much easier to deal with a small problem than having to make a major change to your behaviour. Remember that aggressive behaviour is simply putting yourself above/before others, even though you do not intend to be 'nasty' in any form. Watch your behaviour when you are stressed or very enthusiastic; if you catch yourself behaving aggressively just stop and think:

1. What did you do/say?

   _____

2. What was the result of your aggressive behaviour?

   _____

3. What should you have done/said?

   _____

Now practise saying it aloud (so it sounds natural to you); close your eyes and visualise the encounter with the outcome you wanted.

Next time, be alert to the situation and try to catch yourself before you give in.

**And finally**

Identify three changes you could make to the way you look, move or speak to help yourself be seen as less aggressive:

1. _____

2. _____

3. _____

# 3 Assertive behaviour

*Have a calm and measured presence ...*
*... which is clearly heard, but doesn't dominate.*

Assertiveness involves respecting yourself and demonstrating that respect through clear and honest communication in different situations. It is based on the balance between how you view and treat yourself in relation to how you treat others.

One of the best reasons for being assertive is that you will be less passive or aggressive. You will be more effective in your dealings with others and people will work with you, rather than against you. Your interaction with others will be more rewarding and you will develop a more positive approach to life.

Assertive behaviour involves:

* taking responsibility for your needs, feelings and opinions

    *I'd like to go to Italy this year; how about you?*

    (not *Where would you like to go on holiday? Someone at work said Italy was nice.*)

* saying clearly what you want, but respecting the rights of others (asking, not demanding)

    *I would like to take the last two weeks of June; how will that fit in with you?*

Assertive behaviour also involves demonstrating confidence and a good level of self-respect and self-esteem.

A very few people are lucky enough to be naturally assertive, but even they are likely to face some situations where they feel less confident (or where pressure may make them behave aggressively). Most people develop assertive behaviour through practice. It's a skill, just like asking open questions:

*Terry* felt awkward meeting people; it was hard to make conversation and his efforts seemed to go nowhere. His friend pointed out that this was partly his doing because he asked questions such as 'Did you manage to park?' or 'Did you like the presentation?' These only invited a yes/no answer.

With a bit of thought and practice, Terry developed the art of asking questions such as, 'How did you get on with parking here?' or 'What did you think of the presentation?' As a result, he found he could build conversations.

Assertive communication is like that. The words you use and the way you behave will have an impact on the outcome of the situation, and assertiveness is a behaviour which is likely to achieve good outcomes.

*Terry* also found it difficult to say when he didn't understand an instruction. He tended to keep quiet and just do his best to work out what was wanted. He realised this wasn't a good approach when a lengthy report on improving the car parking situation was rejected because he had focused on design and structural changes to the site. His manager had wanted comparisons of all the alternative ways staff could travel to work and so reduce the number of cars on site.

After a long complaint to his sister, he recognised that he was unhappy, saying that he didn't understand after he'd felt foolish for doing so at school – the result of one teacher putting him down publicly. He felt his manager was at fault for not giving clearer direction, but acknowledged that he had to share the blame because, although he hadn't been certain what was wanted, he didn't ask.

Manager: Terry, can you find out about replacing the computers?

Terry: Do you mean whether we can afford to do it?

Manager: No ... when IT are intending to do it.

# Does 'assertive' describe a person?

No! 'Assertive' describes how that person is behaving at a given time, and there will be many factors that affect that behaviour.

**Elaine** went out with friends who'd met at ante-natal classes eight years before. They had no plans for the evening and, when they met, were discussing where to go. Elaine didn't think twice about suggesting the new Mexican restaurant at the top of town.

*Relaxed in the company of friends, Elaine was easily assertive.*

The following Thursday, the sales team that Elaine had recently joined went for a drink after work. Mid-afternoon, they were discussing where to go. Elaine kept quiet, even though she was really keen to try the new Mexican restaurant.

*In the company of unfamiliar work colleagues, Elaine was passive and waited to see what type of places they liked before commenting.*

Elaine's husband had suggested going out on Saturday and agreed to book cinema tickets. She had asked him twice during the week whether he'd done so, and eventually on Friday snapped that she would do it – the only way to get anything done.

*Aggressive behaviour!*

## But some people seem to be naturally assertive!

Most are not – but they do seem to be. You don't know how they're feeling inside; or that their behaviour in another situation could be very different.

Your behaviour will be influenced by a wide range of factors. For example,

- your childhood
- your schooling
- your work experience
- your conditioning (men don't cry!)
- your past experience of the person you are currently dealing with
- your past experience of the type of person you are dealing with

- your current mood.

## What is the effect on me?

The effect is positive.

- By saying clearly what you want you have a much greater chance of getting it. (Don't complain of tiredness and hope for the offer of a cup of tea – just ask for the cup of tea!) Most people are happy to help you if they know what it is you want.

- Conflicts are less likely because of clear, open communication focused on the needs of both parties.

- By demonstrating self-confidence, you will be perceived as confident and other people will have trust and faith in you and your ability.

- Developing your ability to say 'no' will give you greater control of your workload and time.

- Developing a positive attitude will have a beneficial effect on your general mood.

## What's the effect on the other person?

People like dealing with someone behaving assertively because they know where they stand, what's wanted and where problems lie. Assertive behaviour demonstrates respect for others as well as for self, and people respond well when they feel valued and respected.

## What is the effect on a situation?

Clear communication, and the emphasis on achieving the best possible outcome to a situation, reduces problems.

If you are assertive, people will feel able to talk to you and explain concerns; so little problems are sorted before they become big problems.

- When, or with whom, do you find it easy to be assertive?

- What is it about the person or behaviour that makes it easy?

_____

- What are the three priority situations where you would benefit from a more assertive approach?

_____

# 4 Rights

*Rights are the basis of assertive communication ...*
*... the balance between the rights to give to yourself and to others form the basis of how you behave and communicate.*

Assertive communication is based on the assumption that you give rights to yourself and to others, and the balance between those affects how you behave. These rights are not set in stone and they are not legally enforceable.

They form the basis for your behaviour in that if you take rights for yourself that you do not give to others, you will behave aggressively. If you give rights to others, but do not match this by taking the same rights for yourself, you will behave passively.

**Miriam** *is the administrator for a team of 11, all of whom have conflicting priorities. Miriam finds it almost impossible to say no and, as a result, often has to stay late or take work home. Her team use her as a walking source of reference, interrupting her to ask her for telephone numbers or the name of the person responsible for something. She often wastes time because she isn't given clear instructions and has to muddle through.*

*However, members of the team sometimes offer to help her and there are another two administrators in the office who would help if asked, but they are also very busy. Miriam's immediate response to an offer of help is on the lines of 'I'm fine' 'I've nearly done it' , or 'you've enough to do', and she has never asked the other two for help.*

*Broadly, Miriam is putting the others before herself, she is scared of being seen as unable to cope, isn't taking her needs into account and doesn't want to risk looking stupid.*

All rights stem from the basic, underlying right to be your own person. On the next page are some general rights, in the context of assertiveness, which cause most discussion on training courses.

Read each and give your instant reaction without thinking about it. Then consider the 'Now think about it' section and look for examples/evidence of when you do, or don't, take that right for yourself.

> **Josh** *looked at the first right below (the right to your own feelings, needs and opinions) and immediately ticked 'of course', giving examples of:*
>
> - *arguing that the referee was wrong to award the penalty in the match he and his friends were watching in the pub;*
>
> - *saying that he didn't like musicals because they were too 'happy ever after' (in the company of friends who did like them).*

However, when Josh thought about it, he recognised that he tended to keep quiet about his opinions in front of his manager, even in front of his workmates. He also realised that when he first met someone, he tended to find out what they thought before he gave an opinion.

**I have the right to my own feelings, needs and opinions and to have them respected by others.**

You do not have to justify your opinions to others. People see things differently and it is important to move away from the idea that if one party is right, another must be wrong.

|  | of course | seems reasonable | hmm, not really | no way |
|---|---|---|---|---|
| Instant reaction: | ☐ | ☐ | ☐ | ☐ |

Now think about it:

When/with whom I'm comfortable to express my opinions:

_____

And when I'm not:

_____

When/with whom I'm comfortable to express what I need:

_____

And when I'm not:

_____

When/with whom I'm comfortable to express my feelings:

_____

And when I'm not:

_____

## I have the right to consider my own needs

This does not mean that you insist on doing what you want, when you want it, rather that you take yourself into the equation. How often have you found yourself helping a neighbour and thought, 'Hang on, I was going to meet a friend this afternoon'? It's easy to get swept into doing things for others and completely forgetting what you need and want. You might still help, but it will be a conscious choice.

|  | *of course* | *seems reasonable* | *hmm, not really* | *no way* |
|---|---|---|---|---|
| Instant reaction: | ☐ | ☐ | ☐ | ☐ |

Now think about it:

When I do tend to take my own needs into account:

_____

And when I don't:

_____

## I have the right to ask

It can be uncomfortable to ask for help, for information or explanation and, as a result, we justify ourselves, or drop hints and hope they are taken up. Have you ever said how tired you are, how difficult your day was, in the hope of being made a cup of tea? If you simply said, 'Please could you make me a cup of tea, ' you'd be far more likely to get one.

|  | *of course* | *seems reasonable* | *hmm, not really* | *no way* |
|---|---|---|---|---|
| Instant reaction: | ☐ | ☐ | ☐ | ☐ |

Now think about it:

When/who I feel comfortable to ask:

_____

But not so comfortable when:

_____

## I have the right to be successful

It's easy to accept this in theory, but listen to what goes on around you. Compliments are brushed aside ('I bought it in the charity shop') or deflected ('You should see Suki's presentation'). This usually leads the person giving the compliment to justify it and the whole thing becomes a negative spiral, not the positive that it should be.

|  | of course | seems reasonable | hmm, not really | no way |
|---|---|---|---|---|
| Instant reaction: | ☐ | ☐ | ☐ | ☐ |

Now think about it:

When I feel able to accept a compliment:

_____

And when I don't:

_____

How I tend to respond:

_____

## I have the right to refuse a request

If there is one thing that people look for in assertiveness training, it's help with saying no. People say things like, 'It's difficult ...' or 'I'm very pushed at the moment' but they don't say, 'No, I can't cover reception this afternoon'.

|  | of course | seems reasonable | hmm, not really | no way |
|---|---|---|---|---|
| Instant reaction: | ☐ | ☐ | ☐ | ☐ |

Now think about it:

When I feel able to say no:

And when/with whom I end up saying yes:

## I have the right to make a mistake

Many people operate a double standard over this right, lying awake going over a mistake made earlier in the day, but allowing the mistakes of others, recognising that 'They're new to this', or 'She was under pressure'. No one likes making mistakes, but if you've never made a mistake then you've probably never tried anything new.

|  | of course | seems reasonable | hmm, not really | no way |
|---|---|---|---|---|
| Instant reaction: | ☐ | ☐ | ☐ | ☐ |

Now think about it:

When I feel OK about a mistake I've made:

And when I don't:

Now look back over your answers. Can you draw any conclusions about when you are comfortable in standing up for your rights and/or when you are not? At work or at home? With what type of people? With family, friends or strangers?

_____

_____

_____

> **Gloria's** manager in her first job made her feel inadequate, brushed aside her questions and ridiculed her early mistakes. Now in her mid-forties, Gloria can clearly see that he was a bully, she had been doing the right thing to ask and her mistakes were minor. However, this early experience still influences her behaviour if she doesn't understand something or makes a mistake today.
>
> With some support from a current manager, Gloria talked this through and identified how her early experience still affected her behaviour. She considered how she would feel if her early experience had been positive and how her current behaviour would be different. She practised these behaviours in different situations; for example, making sure that she asked simple, everyday questions in an assertive manner.
>
> Finally, she had to ask a senior manager for a further explanation of some instructions she'd been given. She reminded herself of the assertive communication she'd practised before going on to explain that she'd thought all was well, but now that she'd started the task she had a couple of questions. The manager was fine about it, explaining clearly and thanking her for taking the trouble to check.
>
> Later that evening, Gloria found herself regretting that she'd had to ask and quickly stopped that negative thought, reminding herself of the manager's attitude and response.

## Where do rights come from?

In short, they come from you. Rights are something you take, not something you are given, and are based on your beliefs about yourself, your self-esteem. If you believe that you are not as important as the other person, that people won't like you if you say something, or that you should always put others before yourself, you are likely to behave passively.

Alternatively, if you don't trust others to do the job as well as you, or believe that attack is the best form of defence, or that your project is the most exciting one ever, your behaviour is likely to be aggressive.

The good news is that you can modify negative beliefs with a bit of effort.

## Responsibilities

If you are to behave assertively, it is important to balance the rights you give to yourself with the rights you give to others. If you take more rights than you give, you will behave aggressively. If you give more than you take, you will behave passively.

You therefore have two responsibilities in assertiveness:

- to respect the rights of others
- to assert your rights in a responsible and reasonable manner.

# 5 ... I'm OK

If you are to be assertive and be seen as confident and competent, it is important that you create an overall impression of self-confidence. You need people to generally be aware of you and to have a positive impression of you and your ability.

Non-verbal communication and body language are an essential part of communication. People are considerably more strongly influenced by how we look, speak and move than by the words we use. It is commonly accepted that communication is 53% non-verbal, 38% voice and only 7% words. Even if these figures are heavily influenced by the manner of the research, there is still a significant emphasis on the importance of the non-verbal communication.

The message we send is a combination of our physical stance, movement, gestures, expression and appearance. Just as with our words, the non-verbal communication can send a passive, aggressive or assertive message, and it is important that both verbal and non-verbal messages match if you are to create the impression of confidence.

## Body language

### • Passive body language

Almost all aspects of passive body language centre on messages of submission. These include a shuffling walk, slumped, round-shouldered stance and curled seated position. Fidgeting, constant changes of position, fiddling with jewellery or hair and generally taking up the least possible space will add to the impression. There will be little eye contact, but often a pleading expression and a 'desperate' smile.

## • Aggressive body language

You will give the impression of 'verbal violence' by making yourself look as large as possible (drawing yourself up to your full height, hands on hips). Raised voice with hard tone, a smile but with expressionless eyes, tense jaw muscles, dominant eye contact and invading personal space will add to that impression. Dismissing the person by gestures, by turning away or walking off complete the appearance of aggression.

Tunnel vision caused by pressure or stress will display many of the 'nasty' aspects of the behaviour above, but when it is caused by enthusiasm, it will generally be much more friendly and excitable. Some aspects remain, typically loudness, invasion of personal space and dominant eye contact.

## • Assertive body language

This is where the 'I'm OK' comes in. As the general principle of assertiveness is to feel and demonstrate confidence, there are several aspects of the impression you give that you need to be aware of:

- walking
- talking
- sitting
- standing
- arriving
- leaving
- looking
- dress
- an appearance of calm.

## • Walking

As you sit in your car in the car park, look at people walking. Some shuffle, others stoop, some take small quick steps, others have a long stride. Some dawdle, others look purposeful. Some plod along, others float, like dancers. Look especially for those who appear confident and comfortable; what is it about their stride or movement that gives that impression?

• Describe your walk generally.

• How does it change when you're angry or stressed?

• And when your confidence is low?

• What changes do you want to make to how you walk?

As you next walk across a car park or along a corridor:

• straighten/lengthen spine (imagine being pegged on a line by your ears)

• drop your shoulders (more backwards than forwards or you will stoop)

• make sure you have a moderate stride and breathe comfortably

• set your stomach muscles (not desperately pulling them in, just holding them gently)

Just for fun, as you're walking, try the following:

• lengthen and then shorten your stride – how does it affect how you feel?

• look down from your neck, as though trying to avoid treading in a puddle (feel the pull on your upper spine)

• relax your stomach muscles ... flop!

• turn toes slightly in, and then out.

Try to walk through the foot, from centre back of heel to tip of middle toe, and make sure you don't slam your heel down. Try different heel heights and types of shoe and see what makes you walk with more confidence.

## • Talking

The tone of your voice will have a significant impact on how others perceive your confidence and ability. If you sound as though you know what you are talking about, they will be more inclined to listen; if you sound as though you mean what you say, they are more inclined to accept it.

- *Pitch:* make sure that your voice doesn't get higher when you are under pressure. A lower pitch gives authority.

- *Volume:* you need to speak loudly enough to be heard first time.

- *Speed:* most people gabble under pressure. Practise speaking more slowly, finishing one word before you say the next.

- *Pauses:* make sure your sentences aren't one long gush. A pause here and there adds emphasis and interest, and makes you sound more confident.

- *Warmth:* whilst it's important not to have a fake grin on your face, a smile will add warmth to your tone. (This is also useful when you are on the phone.)

When does your voice/speech let you down (type of situation/mood)?

_____

- What happens to your voice/speech?

_____

- Changes to make when you want/need to:

_____

## A bit of practice

Read a paragraph of a book aloud. As you do so, raise your pitch in stages until it is just below a squeak and then lower it in stages until it is just above a growl. Return to neutral and then increase the volume until it is just below shouting, then decrease it to just above a murmur. Again, return to neutral and try speeding up until you are going as fast as you can, then slow down to 'speaking – to – a – fool' speed. What does this achieve? You've proved that you can manage your voice – so now practise it in conversation. After a while, you will find that you can control and manage your speech in a stressful situation, which might just be the help you need to be seen and heard.

## • Sitting

Whether you're sitting at your desk, in a meeting, at a friend's table or just on the bus, how you sit will send a message. To make sure that it's a positive one:

- Sit to the back of the chair, not perched on the edge.
- Keep your back comfortably straight and your shoulders dropped back.
- Sit on your 'sit bones' and back of thighs, not on the base of your spine.
- Lean forward slightly when you're listening.

Describe your normal seating position in different situations (office, sofa, at a table, in the pub, etc.).

_____

_____

_____

- What messages are you sending?

_____

_____

- What changes would you like to make?

_____

_____

## • Standing

- Stand tall, not super-stretched – just imagine being pegged to a washing line by your ears, then relax a little.

- Roll your shoulders back a few times, then relax them backwards and downwards, but not so far that you stick your chest out!

- Spend most of the time with your weight on both feet.

- Keep your upper body open with hands below waist height.

- Keep your stomach muscles gently 'set', not flopped or overly held in.

- If you're holding papers/files, don't cuddle them or peep over the top.

- You may feel vulnerable, but most people concentrate on your facial expression when they're talking to you, and aren't looking at your body. They're also too busy feeling awkward as well!

Respect people's personal space and be sensitive to those who edge or lean away – they may have a larger area of 'comfort zone' than you have, and are thus feeling that their space is being invaded. Avoid standing over someone who is sitting. If you are discussing something that's on a sheet of paper, try to place yourself alongside the other person, facing the paper together, rather than facing them across the paper.

- Describe your normal stance.

_____

- What message does this send?

_____

- What changes do you want to make?

_____

## • Arriving

Beware of sidling into a room, opening the door a little way, peeping round it and then scuttling to where you intend to sit without looking at anyone. You don't need to make a grand theatrical entrance – it's probably better not to, but first impressions count. You will find it much easier to appear confident if you have got off to a good start.

Always open a door wide enough for both shoulders to arrive in the room at the same time; closing the door behind you (even if it is sprung) will pace your arrival and give you a chance to decide where you are going to sit/stand. If you make eye contact with someone you know, smile a greeting. Move purposefully, but not forcefully to where you plan to go, excusing yourself calmly if you need to squeeze past someone.

## • Leaving

Don't just sneak out from a room, or away from a conversation; always say goodbye. Say it directly to the person you have been talking to if one-to-one. Remember that it is the completion of your interaction with that person, not the start of your interaction with the next. Say a general goodbye, if leaving a group, with a sweep of eye contact around the group. Leave calmly, but with purpose – remember, you are fixing a picture of yourself in everyone's mind, so make sure it is a positive one.

## • Looking

It would be hard to find someone who isn't aware of the importance of eye contact, but that doesn't mean everybody uses it to its best advantage. When you are speaking to someone, really do look at their eyes, and develop the habit of noticing eye colour or shape. Make sure that you keep your facial expression appropriate (it's that which prevents eye contact becoming a stare) and if/when you need to break eye contact, change distance rather than direction (looking away). Practise relaxing the muscles around the eye – it creates a more friendly, open expression. A smile which is clearly for the person on the receiving end has a lot more impact than a general, undirected smile.

Practise 'warm regard': stand in front of a mirror and look yourself in the eye. Now smile, using your mouth only, and you should see how insincere it looks. Smile again, this time letting it extend to your eyes – you should look much friendlier, warmer and more attractive. Now see if you can get something of that 'real' smile in your eyes, without much movement in your mouth ... that's warm regard – looking warmly upon someone.

## • Dress

This has nothing to do with what you spend, but everything to do with how you wear it. It should go without saying that clothes should be clean, pressed and not in need of repair.

However, there are other factors to be taken into account if you want to be seen as confident, competent and in control. It is a fact that people judge by appearances. That doesn't mean that you have to conform to their expectations, but you will have to deal with their response when you don't conform. If you are happy with that, it will not affect your confidence; if you are not happy with their response, then you can be uncomfortable. For example, if you attend a meeting wearing a low-cut shirt, you are likely to attract the gaze of some of the participants. If that doesn't bother you, wear the shirt; if you don't like the attention, wear something else.

However, there is more to clothes than how others see you; they also have a significant impact on how you feel about yourself. Wearing something that you feel good in will have a significant impact on how you stand, sit and walk.

Think about what is in your wardrobe that makes you walk with a spring in your step:

- Items of clothing:

  _____

  _____

- Shoes:

  _____

- Jewellery:

  _____

  _____

- Outerwear:

_____

Think about the clothes you usually wear to work and their impact:

- My normal style of clothes is:

_____

- Why I choose this style:

_____

_____

- What message my style sends:

_____

- What message do I want to send?

_____

_____

- What clothes/style would help me send that message?

_____

Now take that last question and be more specific, thinking about the length/style/cut that you want to aim for when next shopping:

- Skirt:

_____

- Trousers:

_____

- Top:

_____

- Jacket/cardigan:

_____

- Shoes:

  _____

- Colours:

  _____

- Others:

  _____

Try cutting out pictures from magazines that capture the 'look' you would like to create – don't analyse your choices too much, just take the ones you like. When you have 10 or 15 minutes, spread them out on the table and look at them. Identify what you like about them as a whole, and put together the criteria for what you should buy when you have time or money.

## • Don't fidget

On an everyday level, try to avoid any tendency towards twisting a ring, pulling your hair, scratching an eyebrow, clicking a pen, and so on.

When you feel uncomfortable or emotional, it is easy to take refuge in fidgeting: putting your hand over your face, loosening a collar, rubbing an imaginary itch. Apart from being a distraction, these are movements often associated with lying (or at least disguising the truth) and are enough to give someone a sense that something isn't quite right.

### A bit of preparation

If you are facing an awkward situation – maybe a meeting with your manager, a presentation, an interview, or just knowing you will have to say no to someone – think how you would like to be seen. Visualise how you look, how you move, how your voice sounds, and so on. Imagine yourself walking into the room, greeting the person, sitting down, or moving to where you want to stand. Picture the conversation going well, people listening to you and smiling in agreement. It's no guarantee that everything will go smoothly, but you increase the chances by building your confidence. Anyway, there's no point in wasting time and energy imagining it going badly!

# 6 ... I'm positive

Constant criticism and put-downs wear down your self-confidence. But how much of that criticism, how many of the put-downs, come from yourself? For example,

*I really need to lose some weight.*

*I can't do presentations. I go bright red.*

*I'm not a confident driver.*

*I'm hopeless at punctuation.*

*I just  don't understand the formulae in spreadsheets.*

See how these are just passing comments, little asides; however, put together, they combine to show you in a negative light to those around you.  People probably won't notice what you are saying on a conscious level, but the drip, drip of small self-put-downs will combine to give a poor impression. Apart from seeing you as generally less competent, people will take any problems you have, or mistakes you make,  as proof of this perception.

And – send enough negative messages about yourself to yourself, and you will come to believe your own negative publicity!

*Elizabeth is older than her colleagues by about 15 years.  The age gap isn't particularly obvious in terms of her appearance, energy or relationship with her workmates, but she was very upset by hearing herself referred to as the 'office granny'.  There was no obvious malice in the remark and she didn't say anything.  With heightened awareness of her greater years, she realised how often she made passing reference to it with comments like  'I'm in bed with my cocoa by 10', 'senior moment', or 'I know I'm a dinosaur but ...'.*

*Elizabeth recognised that she was more aware of the age difference than she had acknowledged, and the resulting comments were unnecessary additions to the point she was making at the time.  She therefore made a conscious effort to simply cut them out.  She tried to*

pace her speech a little to give herself time to think and made an effort to be aware of what she was saying as she was speaking. She was surprised by how often she was about to make some reference to her age, how much of a habit it had become, and was generally successful in stopping herself.

She hasn't heard another 'office granny' remark and feels generally more confident among her colleagues.

What do you tend to put yourself down for (at work or at home)?

1. _____

2. _____

3. _____

Now take yourself in hand. Every time you are about to put yourself down, just stop. Don't add the negative comment; replace it with a positive one.

For example, replace 'I can't get my head around spreadsheets – could you tell me how to do this formula?' with 'Could you show me how to do this formula?'

or

'I'm learning how to use spreadsheets – could you tell me how to do this formula?'

By being more positive, you will feel better about yourself and the feeling of ability to cope will help reduce stress. If you're not constantly pointing out your self-perceived shortcomings, others will see you as more able. If you need to tackle someone about problems, or deal with difficult behaviours, it will be easier if they see you as a strong person in the first place.

Build your confidence: write down three positive things about your skills at work:

1. _____

2. _____

3. _____

Now three about yourself at home:

1. _____

2. _____

3. _____

Finally, three about your character/personality:

1. _____

2. _____

3. _____

Now that you have something positive to say, use it to balance out the negative thoughts that come to your mind.

'I can't get my head around spreadsheets, but I'm great at handling angry customers'.

Now, return to those areas where you tend to put yourself down. Note the response you tend to make and then rewrite the script.

1. Situation 1:

_____

2. I tend to say/do:

_____

3. A more positive response would be:

_____

_____

1. Situation 2:

_____

2. I tend to say/do:

_____

3. A more positive response would be:

_____

_____

1. Situation 3:

_____

2. I tend to say/do:

_____

3. A more positive response would be:

_____

_____

Now practise it aloud a few times until you sound natural.

## • Compliments

How often have you responded to a compliment with a negative comment, or just brushed it off?

 'Well done with the presentation.'

'It was awful; I could feel myself going red.'

 'That shirt looks great'

'Oh, it's only from the charity shop.'

The problem with this type of response is that the person paying the compliment feels they have to reinforce it, which encourages the recipient to play it down even further.

 'Well done with the presentation'

'It was awful; I could feel myself going red.'

'It didn't show.'

'I could feel it, and I kept looking down at my notes.'

'That shirt looks great.'

    *'Oh, it's only from the charity shop.'*

'The colour really suits you.'

    *I just need to lose a bit of weight so it doesn't gape.'*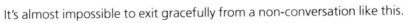

It's almost impossible to exit gracefully from a non-conversation like this.

## Accept a compliment gracefully

A short, clear 'thank you' makes both parties feel good; add a positive if you want to

'That shirt looks great.'

    *'Thank you, it's one of my favourites.'*

'Well done with the presentation.'

    *'Thank you – they seemed supportive.'*

Keep it positive. If you hear yourself adding a negative, turn it round to end on a positive.

'That shirt looks great.'

    *'I got it at the charity shop – I was really pleased with it.'*

Keep the compliment, don't throw it back.

    *'You're looking great as well.'*

Leave out other people who have nothing to do with it; they are irrelevant.

    'Well done with the presentation.'

    *'Thank you ~~but did you see – Jean did hers without notes~~.'*

Look at the person paying you a compliment, and smile. Avoid diffident shrugs or turning your body away in embarrassment.

## • A positive approach to conversation

Listen actively with good eye contact, open expression and body position, and full attention. Periodically summarise what the other person has said; this demonstrates you're listening and is more likely to keep them 'with' you, rather than 'against' you. It also often shortens communication because once someone feels they've been heard, they are less likely to return to the point.

> 'So you feel it's not worth opening between Christmas and New Year. I know we don't do much business then, but there is the occasional call and it would be a shame to miss an order. Is there a way that we could minimise the cost of staffing over that time?'

This is particularly important where you hold opposing views.

> 'I can see that it would save money ... and we certainly need to; I'm concerned about the impact on staff morale.'

## • General positive communication

Negativity is not only self-put-downs, it can be a whole communication style. Listen to people around you; a lot of the phrasing is negative. It's not only verbal communication; look at reports, letters and e-mails and you'll find the same applies.

> 'She's not in the office this afternoon.'

> 'I can't do that until Friday.'

> 'I can only send six.'

> 'You can't have an appointment until tomorrow.'

> 'We only have three qualified staff.'

> 'The scheme is not available to those with under five years' experience.'

None of the examples above would necessarily cause a serious problem, but if they were phrased differently, the tone would be a much more positive one.

*'She's not in the office; she'll be back tomorrow morning.'* (or, *'Can I help?'*)

*'I can do that on Friday.'*

*'I can send six.'*

*'You can have an appointment tomorrow.'*

*'We have three qualified staff.'*

*'The scheme is available to those with five or more years' experience.'*

## Be generally positive

It's not that you should turn yourself into Pollyanna, always happy and looking for things to be happy about, but try not to do the opposite! Try to find something positive to say about the weather, the new system, the office reorganisation. This not only has an impact on how others see you, but can have a surprisingly uplifting effect on your mood and attitude.

It also means that when you do need to raise problems, your concerns are more likely to be recognised because you are not always whingeing!

## Don't let other people put you down

Remember that no one can put you down without your permission. Put-downs vary from minor comments to the truly horrendous that need to be tackled as a separate issue (see Chapter 12 on dealing with negative behaviour/problems).

First, make sure that you are not taking something as a put-down when it simply isn't meant that way.

*Andy's Monday had not been great; late in the afternoon he passed Carole, a colleague he greatly respected and admired, in the corridor and she completely ignored him. Andy was upset and hurt – he had worked hard on a project for Carole the previous month and had been sincerely thanked (he'd thought). This incident preyed on his mind for a few days and he was questioning what he might have done wrong, or what he had done to cause offence. On Thursday, Andy attended a meeting and found himself next to Carole, who greeted him warmly and asked about his current project. As she told him about a horrendous meeting she had attended on Monday afternoon, he realised that she hadn't ignored him intentionally, she'd simply been thinking about something else and not seen him.*

**Tracy** *worked hard at a presentation she had to make and was relieved when it went well. Her manager thanked her, commenting that she obviously hadn't found it easy. Tracy didn't hear much of the remainder of the conversation, as she realised that her nerves had obviously shown and the occasional slip had been clearly noticeable. She was upset for a couple of days before resolving to approach her manager for guidance as to what she should have done differently. Her manager was amazed: she had thought the presentation excellent, but knew how nervous Tracy had been the night before when she'd found her in the office at 6.30 still working on it. What was meant as a compliment had been seen in a very different light.*

*Some put-downs are more serious and may well need to be dealt with as a separate issue. However, you might wish to deal with them on a day-to-day basis to make sure they don't wear you down.*

**Lesley** *was a community matron. She was the only member of the team who worked part-time, combining the job with care of her two young children. Once a month she attended the team meeting and often found herself on the receiving end of barbed comments from Elaine, one of the other matrons. Over time she had contributed less and less, and now was looking for excuses not to attend. Eventually she confided in her team leader, explaining that she didn't want to take formal action but could not see how to proceed. After some support and a few practice sessions, she went to a meeting prepared:*

Lesley:   *How would it work if we did the paperwork at the start of the shift, not the end, and then went out on the road when rush-hour is over?*

Elaine:   *That would never work!*

Lesley:   *I'd like to try it for a week in my area – is that OK with everyone?*

| | |
|---|---|
| *Lesley:* | *How do you do the spreadsheet?* |
| *Elaine:* | *Don't you worry yourself about it. We do it in the afternoons when you've gone home.* |
| *Lesley:* | *I'd still like an idea of how it would work.* |

### • Start and finish your day on a positive

Finish each day by reviewing two or three good things that happened; start the next with two or three things to look forward to. You might even want to find your own mantra (for example, 'I'm a confident, competent person and I can deal with whatever life throws at me today') and see what effect it has.

# 7 ... I'm calm

'I'm stressed' is a common complaint. The word 'stress' is used to describe anything from a bad day to serious physical and mental problems.

Stress is a response to pressure. *Specific pressure*, for example a deadline, is generally a *good* thing. It is what keeps you working productively and efficiently and most people will have found that when the pressure is off, they achieve much less. However, there is also the *general pressure* caused by trying to be everything to everybody, to be a good partner, parent, relation, friend, child, worker, manager, etc. This type of pressure can quickly build to become stress.

There are two types of stress. One is the effect of a major event in your life (divorce, a house move, bereavement); the other is general stress, the result of a build-up of pressure to the point where it affects your wellbeing. Stress is a bad thing, however you look at it.

**Your body**

Your body responds to stress by releasing glucose and adrenaline, the digestive system eases up and the heart pumps blood to the essential organs and muscles (the 'fight or flight' response). This is an essential response when you are facing a physical threat, but is of little help when the cause of your stress is the announcement of redundancies, for instance.

This short-term response does not last long, and your body returns to normal when the threat has passed. However, if you face continuing stressful situations of the general kind, your body is in continuous readiness and this will deplete your resources, leaving you vulnerable to illness.

**Your behaviour**

Stress is likely to make you short-tempered, sharp-voiced and impatient. Your concentration is likely to suffer too, making it difficult to settle to a task. You become more withdrawn and inward looking, focusing on yourself and your problems.

## Your mood

Stress makes you feel anxious, overwhelmed and unable to cope; it may seem not worth even trying to do something, as you know you won't be able to complete it. This feeling of uselessness and failure, perhaps compared with the perceived greater skills of others, can make you feel negative, miserable and full of worries and woe.

## What you achieve

Whilst pressure helps you achieve more by keeping you focused, stress generally leads to you being less productive. You are more likely to make mistakes, which then take time to correct – so other tasks pile up. The worry leads to lack of sleep and tiredness which, in turn, leads to being less efficient, the work piles up and mistakes are again made – a vicious circle.

## Are your stressors inside or outside?

Inside stressors include taking on more than you can cope with, perfectionism, and not looking after yourself physically. Outside stressors include difficult colleagues, insufficient training and excessive working hours.

What makes you feel stressed?

_____

_____

What is the effect on your body?

_____

_____

What is the effect on your mood?

_____

_____

How do you behave when stressed?

_____

_____

There are only two ways to get on top of stress: reduce the amount of it or increase your ability to deal with it. Most of this book is concerned with the latter because increased self-confidence and assertiveness are closely related to improved communication and taking control. However, there are a few simple things that will help you in the short term when you are stressed.

## Walk away from it!

No, don't run away, just walk. Even if it is only a circuit of the car park, walk steadily with a straight back and breathe in steadily, filling your lungs, pause and then breathe out. When you are about three-quarters of the way round, decide what one thing you are going to do next, then return and get down to it.

## Small bites, chewed properly and swallowed!

Not food, but workload. Break tasks down into manageable chunks and then, when you start something, be clear about the end-point and do everything you can to get there before you leave it (see 'I'm in control'). If you are interrupted, deal with the interruption then return to what you were doing and finish it, or get to a suitable stop point, before you move on.

## And on to food ... lunch break

There are two parts to this: 'lunch' and 'break'. First the lunch – there are plenty of articles and books that are dedicated to food for energy and health, but in general:

- Eat lunch. Just as a car will grind to a halt if you are so short of time that you do not stop to get fuel, your body (and mind) need a fuel stop.

- Avoid stodgy comfort food which will weigh you down and divert your body's energy to the digestive system.

- Make sure you get the nutrients you need. For example, a dressed salad of lettuce with a few croutons won't weigh you down and feels like a healthy option. However, it won't provide you with the fuel you need either. Add some tuna or chicken and some vegetables which are rich in vitamins (e.g. carrots, peppers, broccoli), and top with nuts rather than croutons, so your lunch feels more satisfying and will provide more energy. If you need more 'bulk', just add a wholemeal roll.

And the 'break':

- It is so easy to just grab a sandwich and carry on, feeling that you are saving time by not stopping. It is a false economy, as tiredness will catch up with you later, making you prone to mistakes and less efficient generally. There is no point in saving half an hour at lunch, if you lose 45 minutes in the afternoon.

- Change of scene: get away from your desk obviously, to avoid people coming to you with work or problems; less obviously, to give your eyes a change of focus and your brain a change of scene.

- Try to get some movement into your break. Ideally something purposeful, like walking to a target, such as the end of the road, rather than just wandering around a shop. Walking a bit faster gets your heart-rate up and encourages you to breathe properly.

- Take a voice recorder (or your mobile phone if it records speech). Once your brain and body relax a bit, you will often find you remember something that would otherwise be forgotten … or just have a good idea. Being able to record it, means you can let it go and carry on (rather than adding to your stress level by trying to remember it!).

## It's not only plants that need water

It's hard to avoid all the encouragement to drink litres of water a day, but it is really important to keep your body hydrated. It will help keep you alert; it also helps avoid headaches.

## De-stress exercises

Try all, or some, of the following:

- Breathe! Feelings of stress tend to lead to shallow breaths, using the upper part of the lung only. Straighten your back, set abdominal muscles, breathe fully into your lungs and exhale fully.

- Roll a small ball forward and backwards under your feet (golf ball size is usually best, but ideally a slightly softer one).

- Raise your shoulders towards your ears, hold for a couple of seconds and release; repeat a few times, then roll shoulders forward and backward a couple of times. Finish by pushing shoulders down (straight-backed) and release. Try to keep the movements smooth and don't forget to breathe!

- Stretch up: sit straight in your chair, link your fingers and stretch to the ceiling, breathing in. Hold it for a few seconds, then bring your arms back down to your side, breathing out.

## What's worrying you?

Stress and worry are often spoken of together, but they are different things. Stress is the build-up of pressure to the point where it has a negative impact; worry is generally to do with what might happen. Worrying wastes your time and will add to the pressure you are under, contributing to stress.

What worries you? What causes your stomach to sink? What comes to mind when you wake in the night, or comes up in conversation repeatedly without being solved?

_____

_____

_____

_____

_____

_____

## Make a worry note

If you tend to spend time worrying, just keep a pad with you and note anything that you find you are worrying about. Now it's noted, get on with what you were doing and you can come back to it later.

Find some time when you won't be interrupted, and for each worry:

- define exactly what it is
- identify the worst thing that could happen
- decide what you would do if this worst thing did happen
- work out whether there are any steps you can take to prevent it happening and, if so, actively plan to take them. If not
- don't waste time worrying, wait until it happens, then deal with it
- remind yourself of the positive, what is the best possible outcome and ask yourself if there is anything you can do to increase the chances of it happening.

For example:

'I am worried about my son's driving test. The worst thing that is likely to happen is that he'll fail – if he does, he'll have to take it again. I can help by taking him driving every evening this week – he might pass!'

or

'There's nothing I can do, so I'll consciously not dwell on it – put it out of my mind every time I think of it.'

Now try it.

I'm worried about:

_____

The worst that could happen is:

_____

_____

Are there any steps I could take to prevent the worst?

_____

_____

And the best that could happen?

_____

Remind yourself of the three (or more) things that you want to remember to do to reduce the stress, or its impact on your life:

1. _____

2. _____

3. _____

# 8 ... I'm in control

Many people feel they simply have too much to do, leaving them stressed and rushing from one task to another. As a result, mistakes are made and things get forgotten.

The clear boundaries between work and home life have become blurred. Technology means that we can answer e-mails on the bus, or be contacted whilst walking down the road for a sandwich. As a result, there are fewer breaks in the day for gathering our thoughts.

Job descriptions have become both more detailed and more vague. Take the role of 'administrator'; in addition to a range of specific tasks come phrases like 'to support', which is wide open to interpretation, and there's always that last 'and any other duties ...' line which can encompass anything. Cuts in staff levels mean that work is shared out to the point where people feel on the edge of complete meltdown.

It is important to be in control for a variety of reasons:

- What you control, you can manage.

- If you are seen to be in control, people will have confidence in you and your work, and be more likely to leave you in peace to get on with it.

- If you feel in control, you will suffer less stress.

### • So how do I take control?

*The first stage is to accept that there will always be parts of the day that you cannot control: the telephone call just as you are adding up a list of figures, the interruption when you are in the middle of writing a difficult letter, the need to help someone with a work crisis. The important thing is how you respond to those interruptions; consider the following snapshots from Farhana's day:*

*When **Farhana** arrived, her manager was waiting for her with some urgent preparation needed for two presentations, one this morning, one slightly different version in the early afternoon.*

*She immediately did the work on the first presentation and gave it to her manager on a memory stick. She then saved it under a different name ready for editing for the later one. She put the papers immediately beside her computer on the 'absolutely essential' pile. (Good practice: she did what was essential immediately and was managing the remainder.)*

*A colleague rang to ask for some help with a spreadsheet he was doing for a meeting at 11. He was over-wrought, having been struggling with it for over an hour.*

*Farhana responded with 'Of course, I'll come over in ten minutes.' This meant she could complete the e-mail she was writing. (Good practice: she recognised the urgency of the task, but didn't automatically respond to her colleague's stress by stopping what she was doing in the middle of a task that would only take a few minutes to complete. She also would find it easier to close the conversation with him because she could leave, rather than getting him to leave her office. She took control of her use of time.)*

*A crisis meant Farhana had to ring around and find her manager immediately.*

*She stopped typing the minutes immediately, but before she put them to one side, she noted that item seven was the next to be drafted. (Good practice: she knew where to start next time – rather than where she stopped. It's only a different way of looking at the same thing, but is more positive and forward looking.)*

## • Three techniques for staying in control

### 1: Use a scheduled task list

Don't use your brain for storage. In a pressured working environment the brain tends to be good at processing information, but less good at remembering things, usually recalling them randomly and often at the wrong moment. So, use your brain for thinking, planning, designing and a task list for storage. However, if a task list is used ineffectively, it will take more time than it saves. Most people read the list from the top and do the most important/interesting thing they come to first – a problem if there's something more important further down the list. In addition, a long list is demoralising and time is wasted rewriting part-done lists.

A task list is, by definition, in the order in which things were given to you or remembered. This is in conflict with the way it should be used – in order of priority. The problem is that we generally don't actually do the task until it <u>has</u> to be done, so a long list builds up. Take a different approach – try noting tasks in the order of outcome, not input.

> **Shavi** was asked on Tuesday to put together some statistics for a meeting on Friday. He decided that the task would actually have to be done on/by Thursday afternoon ... so he put it on Thursday's list (not Tuesday's). Now he can forget about it until it has to be done.

> His colleague **Una** received an e-mail on Thursday 2nd asking her to prepare an agenda for the Strategy Group Meeting on the 28th. She put reminders on her task list for the 18th (ask participants for items), 21st (draw up the agenda – participants' items, things from previous minutes – also 21st see her manager to get it approved), and 22nd (to finalise attachments and send it).

> **Shavi** was later asked to prepare a presentation for the meeting on Friday. He again went to put it on the task list for Thursday, but realised that he wouldn't have time to prepare both presentation and statistics that day, so he scheduled in the presentation for Wednesday.

This system works just as well on paper as electronically; try using a page-a-day diary.

### 2: Manage work by using a 'letterbox'

Imagine coming home at night to find a pile of post that has come through your letterbox. Most of it will be junk mail; some will be bills, bank statements, etc; maybe one will be a personal letter. The junk mail will probably end up straight in the bin, the invoices and bank statements will be put in the appropriate place to be dealt with when you pay the bills, and the personal letter is likely to be read immediately.

Now think about using the same process for work and/or paper that comes across your desk. Stop and calmly review each task as it arrives (or is remembered). Make sure that you look at everything once, properly, and make an immediate decision about it:

- If it's to be binned, throw it away now.

- If it's to be filed, file it, or put it with the other papers to be filed.

- If it's to be read, put it with the other documents you keep to be read on the train (or wherever).

- If it's to be actioned, ask yourself:

   ○ is it a simple task (a task is a single job – e.g. book Eastbourne Travelodge for next week)?

   ○ will it take less than, say, three minutes? If yes, just do it now.

   If it will take longer:

   ○ decide when it will need to be done and put it in your scheduled task list for the appropriate day;

   ○ is it a multi-task (made up of several tasks – for example, 'draw up agenda' will involve getting items, collating papers, checking previous minutes, liaison with chairperson, drafting, sending)? If so, plan it; either break it down into its parts and put each item in the scheduled list, or it may be more appropriate to plan later, in which case remind yourself to do the planning with a note in your scheduled list.

### 3: Manage interruptions

Interruptions fall into two categories. Time-takers are interruptions that are related to your work. Because they are what you are paid to deal with, you cannot avoid them, but they should be streamlined to reduce the time they take.

Time-wasters are, as they sound, people or calls that you just shouldn't be involved in. For example, people stopping by your desk because you sit near the door, or asking you for phone numbers instead of looking them up. These are the interruptions that should be eliminated, or at least reduced.

- Deal with **time-takers** by:
  - ○ getting down to business quickly.

    For example, replace

    *'Hello Judi, how are you?'* with *'Hello Judi, what can I do for you?'*

  - ○ stating a time limit at the outset.

    For example,

    *'Have you got a minute?'*

    *'I've got around three – is that enough or shall I call you this afternoon?'*

  - ○ bringing conversations to a close by summarising the discussion or action to be taken and confirming with the other person.

  - ○ supporting your closing tone with non-verbal behaviour, e.g. collecting papers together, closing a file, etc.

  - ○ visiting others, rather than inviting them to your office. That way you have control over when to go.

- Deal with **time-waster**s by:
  - ○ investing time in preventing them; brief  the switchboard on where to direct calls.

  - ○ trying to avoid getting involved in the first place. It is easier to say at the outset that you have not got time, rather than waiting until the person is half-way through the detail.

  - ○ not looking up, unless someone arrives at your desk.

    Eye contact ➡ smile ➡ greeting ➡ conversation = time waster.

    Learn to say no!

In what areas are other people controlling you/your work?

_____

_____

What effect does this have on you and your efficiency?

_____

_____

Identify three things you could do to get more control of your day:

1. _____

2. _____

3. _____

# 9 ... I'm asking for

Sometimes it's so easy to ask, that you don't give it a second thought. On other occasions, you might find yourself putting it off, or having to steel yourself to approach someone. It might be their attitude, or your previous experience of asking them. Or it might be that you are embarrassed by your lack of knowledge, by needing help, or by having failed to understand something the first time you were told.

If you feel awkward, you are likely to show this by being hesitant or justifying the reasons for asking; alternatively you might sound abrupt.

Either way, it is important to remember that you have a clear right to ask, but also that they have the right to a clear request and to refuse you if they need to.

Think of an awkward a situation.

I don't like asking (name or type of person/type of situation):

_____

_____

As a result I:

_____

_____

This makes me look/seem:

_____

_____

## • Make clear what's required

Asking for some help with a presentation could be anything from five minutes changing the font size to an afternoon of preparation and guidance. When you ask, make it clear what is required.

e.g.         'Would you be able to proofread my slides for tomorrow's presentation? There are about 20 of them.'

'Please could you type this [showing it] report by Friday?'

## • Ask, don't hint

Have you ever heard yourself hinting about what you need, and then being disappointed when the hint is missed.

e.g.      'It's been an awful day ... I'm too tired to move.'

> *means* ... 'Please could you put the kettle on?'

'I'm concerned that this report is too long.'

> *means* ... 'Would you be able to have a look at it for me?'

## • Be direct

People like to know what they're being asked to take on, so questions like 'Have you got half an hour this evening?' or 'Would you be able to give me a hand?' are likely to be met with suspicion.

Clarify in your own mind what it is you need, then ask directly for it.

e.g.      *'Would you be able to take an early lunch today, so I can go at one o'clock?'*

> *'Please could you ask Jenni to ring me when she gets in?'*

> *'Sam, I need the complaints figures for the board meeting – could you get them done by Thursday?'*

## • Give a reason if you must, but don't justify

The more reasons and justifications you give for your request, the less likely you are to get a positive response. People get confused or bored, and switch off and miss the point you are making. See how much less successful the following requests are likely to be than the ones in the previous section:

*'Dan, my sister's just rung – she's in town today. I haven't seen her for weeks. Would you be able to take an early lunch today? I wouldn't normally ask, but she's not been well and I do want to*

*catch up with her, and if I can go at 1.00 we can have half an hour when she's out of the dentist.'*

*'I've just had Mike on the phone; he's not pleased about the figures we put together. I'm hoping that Jenni can come up with some background information – please could you ask her to ring me when she gets in? Will it be before three?"*

*'Sam, I need the complaints figures for the board meeting – could you get them done by Thursday? I know you've a lot on, what with Alex being away, but it is really important that we put together something to impress them after last month's problems. If you could just do it in draft – or give me the data and I'll have a go at them.'*

## • Don't plead and grovel

Most people aren't interested in how useless you feel; they'll just switch off.

e.g.        instead of
'I know I haven't been here long ... and it was very different at my last job ... I hope you don't mind me asking, but would it be possible to do the report using data from the spreadsheets for the charts?'

try        *'I've been looking at the monthly report – would it be OK if I created the charts from the figures in the spreadsheets?'*

## • Don't flatter them into submission

Flattering someone so that they feel they can't let you down is being manipulative, and therefore aggressive. Phrases like 'As you are the PowerPoint genius ...' or 'I'd be so grateful for some advice from a real expert ' may get you a 'yes', but if they're not committed, they may be resentful, or let you down later.

## • Let them say no

Having asked, be quiet and let the other person answer. If they refuse, accept it gracefully and without trying to apply pressure. Remember that most people don't like saying no and so may appear awkward or abrupt, so you might want to plan what to say if you are refused.

 'Could you go to the finance meeting for me next Monday?'

> *'Oh, I'm sorry; I would, but we've got that big presentation on Monday afternoon and I have to work with John on it all morning.'*

'No problem – I'll just send apologies.'

You might want to be sensitive to signs that the other person is unwilling – remember again that most people do not like saying no, and will talk themselves into doing something they don't want to. Although you might be keen for them to agree, it is better to find out at this stage if there is a problem.

 'Could you go to the finance meeting for me next Monday?'

> *'Umm, let me think ... I suppose so; I can prepare the presentation over lunch.'*

'That doesn't sound like a good idea – it's your first one, isn't it?'

> *'Yes, but it's a team one ... I'm just doing a bit of it.'*

'No, don't worry, I'll just send apologies; it doesn't matter if we miss one meeting.'

Think of some of the people you find difficult to approach.

Person:

_____

Why they're difficult to approach:

_____

How I tend to ask/behave:

_____

How I will do it in future:

_____

_____

Person:

_____

Why they're difficult to approach:

_____

How I tend to ask/behave:

_____

How I will do it in future:

_____

_____

_____

Person:

_____

Why they're difficult to approach:

_____

How I tend to ask/behave:

_____

How I will do it in future:

_____

_____

_____

# 10 ... I'm saying no

Probably the single most common reason for an interest in assertiveness is wanting to say no. If we don't say it, we end up with too much to do, involved in things that don't interest us, stressed and resentful. Because it is difficult to say it, we waste time with excuses and justifications and find ourselves pushed into saying yes, with the attempt to refuse either not heard, or ignored.

Consider the type of situations when you would like to say no: at work (e.g. staying late), at home (e.g. Sunday lunch with the in-laws):

1. _____
2. _____
3. _____
4. _____
5. _____

## • Why is it so difficult?

People give a variety of reasons for finding it difficult, but the most common include:

- wanting to please, to be liked
- not wanting to be seen as not able to cope
- feeling guilty
- thinking that no one else can do it
- 'I always say yes'
- feeling that they assume I'll say yes and don't hear me.

Why is it difficult for you to say no?

1. 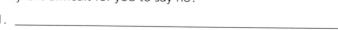 _____

2. _____

3. _____

We often fail to listen to our inner voice, the one which is telling us that this is not what we want to do. We are more worried about what others will think of us than about what we need and want. As a result, there's a hesitation in the refusal that ends up with us giving in and resenting it, or wasting time worrying about how to get out of the situation later.

## • Why not saying no is a bad idea

If you keep saying yes, you will end up with more work than you can handle. This is when mistakes are made and things get forgotten which will reflect badly on you. You will end up working through breaks and staying late, facing the real risk of suffering stress.

You are likely to feel put-upon and blame others (rather than taking responsibility for your own actions). The pressure is likely to make you snappy and bad tempered, which will not be good for your relationships with colleagues and customers.

*You can also cause others to feel guilty, as **Winnie** did when she asked her colleague, Ed, if he could prepare some slides for a presentation. He agreed and did the job by the agreed deadline. Winnie later discovered that he had stayed at work until 7.00, as he had some data to process for a meeting the following morning. Winnie felt guilty and awkward with Ed.*

*Winnie could just as easily have been irritated and frustrated that Ed hadn't told her – another negative outcome.*

## • When you need to say no

You will need to say no if the request is unreasonable. At one end of the scale, this is quite easy: if you were asked to rob a bank, you probably wouldn't find it difficult to refuse. However, many unreasonable requests are much more mundane: to cover reception at lunchtime, or to work late, and these are the ones that are difficult for many to refuse.

Even with mundane requests, it is easier to refuse when you just can't do the task; for example, working late when you have a child to collect. It is harder when it is something you could do, but you really don't want to.

You may also want to say no to things that are not your job or not within your hours. In today's world, with fewer staff available, it can seem churlish and petty, but everyone has a limit to what they can take on.

It would be a sad world if we didn't put ourselves out sometimes, help each other when needed, or do a favour for a friend or colleague; but consider the situations below:

**Toby** is working late. It's 6.45 and he's alone in the office, putting the finishing touches to the music for an advertising jingle that is to be recorded first thing next morning. He had put aside the afternoon to work on it, but spent 90 minutes helping a colleague who was struggling with an unfamiliar computer program (he ended up re-writing the piece) and, later, helping a member of his team to assemble a team to deal with a problem.

**Vanya** is lying awake in the early hours. She's agreed to go on a girls' weekend' with colleagues from the office and has agreed to drive them. It is much further than she usually drives and involves the motorway, where she feels nervous and flustered. She doesn't really want to go, and certainly doesn't want to drive.

**Sarah** is preparing for a presentation she's to make on behalf of her manager, who has gone away for a long weekend. It is not part of her job; she's only done two before and they were some time ago in a previous job and were not successful. She hasn't been trained, and her manager just gave her the slides with no briefing, pointing out that she's been working on the project for three months, so knows all that is needed.

All three of the characters above needed to say no!

When have you recently said yes, when you wanted to say no? Why did it happen?

Situation 1.

Why didn't you say no?

_____

Situation 2.

_____

Why didn't you say no?

_____

Situation 3.

_____

Why didn't you say no?

_____

Look at the situations and reasons above. What common threads can you draw? (Is it a particular person, a type of person or situation, something about your mood at the time?)

## • **Where it goes wrong**

You will find it harder to get your no heard and accepted if you bury it in excuses and justification. You will also find it harder if your voice is saying no, but your body language is saying either yes, or 'push a little harder and I'll cave in'! Our discomfort can give us a torrent of words, an inappropriate smile and pleading body language which all weaken our message.

You may find that you are so unused to taking responsibility for yourself and making decisions about what you want and don't want to do, that it is a big step. It will almost certainly take some thought, a bit of preparation and quite a lot of practice.

## • **So say no**

### Use the word

It is easy to say anything but no. We use phrases like 'It's difficult', 'I'm really busy today', 'Ewen doesn't like me to be out of the office' or 'I have to get this done'. The problem is that the other person hears 'It's difficult ... but I'll manage' or 'I'm really busy today ... but I'll fit it in', and so on.

Obviously a blunt no will seem rude and will be almost impossibly uncomfortable to say, but make sure the word appears in your refusal.

*'No, I can't today – I have to leave at 4.00.'*

*'I need to take an early lunch break so no, I can't cover at 12.'*

## Zip it!

Having refused, stop talking and don't just hang about waiting to be over-ruled. If you carry on, you'll talk yourself into it.

*'No, I can't today – I have to leave at 4.00 ... I know I've stayed before but I need to be home for 5.30 and I have to collect Daisy from nursery. I hope you can find someone to help – they don't like it if I'm late. Normally I would ... I suppose I could stay until 4.15 if that would help'.*

## Don't apologise

You haven't done anything wrong. The problem we face is that 'sorry' has two uses in English, one to apologise and one to express regret.

*'I'm sorry I forgot to ring yesterday.' (apology)*

*'I'm sorry, I can't stay late tonight.' (regret)*

The word 'sorry' has become a social lubricant, used to oil the wheels of conversation – often when we're uncomfortable with what we're saying. However, it sends a message of apology to ourselves, as well as those we're refusing, and that tone of apology/regret can make it easier for them to push.

Try to remove it from your refusals – you might like to replace it with the person's name.

*'~~I'm sorry~~ Sarah, no, I can't – I have to leave at 4.30.'*

*'~~I'm sorry Dan~~, I need to take an early lunch break so no, I can't cover.'*

## Give a reason if you must, but don't justify

In fact, there is no need to give a reason; if you are paid to work until 4.30, you should not have to justify why you can't work later. While you work towards that, concentrate on limiting what you say.

> *'No, I can't today – I have to leave at 4.30 … I need to be home for 5.30 and I have to collect Daisy from nursery. I hope you can find someone to help – they don't like it if I'm late. Normally I would, but I've promised to take my sister out – she's got her driving test next week, so we're going out every night, and she can only go before she goes to work at 7.30.'*

The reason you can't work late is that you have to leave at 4.00; the rest is justification. It's like adding tonic to gin, adding more just weakens the flavour! Much better to keep it simple.

> *'No, I can't today – I have to leave at 4.30.'*

Identify a situation where you might want to say no.

Now try three different ways to word your refusal (include the word 'no', omit the word 'sorry').

1. _____

2. _____

3. _____

Now try saying all three aloud and edit the one that sounds most natural. Now practise it in different voice tones, at different speeds, and so on. Finally, use it!

## • It's my job, so I can't say no

Sometimes, perhaps often, the request is something is something you are paid to do, which makes refusal even more uncomfortable.

> *'Could you tidy up the slides for my presentation to the board?'*

> *'Can you minute the meeting this afternoon?'*

*'Please can you find Mr Jackson's notes?'*

Assuming you are paid to do the tasks above, you could be forced to take them on. Most people are reasonable; if you respond appropriately, they will accept a refusal, or work with you.

In this situation, you will almost certainly have to give a reason, so keep it simple, clear and short. You might feel you have to use the word 'sorry' as you are genuinely apologising.

*'I'm sorry, I can't Rashid – I've never used PowerPoint.'*

*'We have to get this mailing out by the end of the day and I just can't take an hour out for the meeting.'*

You may also need to give the person the choice of what you do.

*'I can certainly go and look for them, but I won't be able to get your report finished by lunchtime – is that OK?'*

## • Yes/No

Sometimes it is difficult to say no because part of the task is perfectly possible; it's the timescale, or the manner of doing it, that is the problem.

*'Could you get the figures done by the end of the week?'*

*'Could you add Mrs Phipps to your list of visits for today?'*

*'Can you type this for me now?'*

In the examples above, it is fine to do the figures, but not this week; or no problem to see Mrs Phipps, but your list is full today.

In situations like this you need to say yes to part of the request and no to the other. Try to keep it positive and come up with an alternative, rather than leave it up to the other person.

*'I can certainly do them, but it will be Monday afternoon.'*

*'Yes, I'll see her – I can add her to my list tomorrow.'*

*'No problem, I'll do it as soon as I've sent these e-mails'.*

Identify a situation where you might want to use yes/no.

_____

Think how you can phrase it and practise until it sounds
natural.

_____

_____

Don't forget to practise it aloud!

# 11 ... I really mean no

In a perfect world, your no would be heard and accepted. In the real world, that is not always the case at first. Sometimes it is because the other person is so used to you saying yes that they don't even hear the no. Others are so swept up in what they are doing that they just don't notice you are not with them; and there are some who resort to various tactics to try to turn your no into a yes.

In the case of those who just didn't hear, or take on board, your refusal, you need to deal with it quickly. Once the task has been left with you, it is harder to pass it back. Call the person back, probably using their name to get attention; keep your voice tone light and warm – treat it as a misunderstanding, not an attempt to get at you. Once you have their attention, explain again, using the same reason. If there is paper involved, you may find it easier to hand it back, rather than asking them to take it back.

'Thanks for sorting the figures – can you send them to everyone in the quality forum before you go?'

   'I can't, I'm just on my way out of the door.'

'Thanks.'

   'Angela ... I can't do it this afternoon, I'm on my way home.'

'Can't you just do it before you go?'

   'No, my computer is off and I have to go now.'

'Oh ... OK – leave it until the morning.'

## • Types of persistence

Imagine a colleague asks you to stay late to help with a big mailing that has to be sent out today. You've refused because you have to leave on time (you are meeting a friend who is facing a major operation).

**Pleading**  *'Oh, please – there's no one else who can do it.'*

Respond by simply restating the refusal.

> *'I know, but I have to be away on time today.'*

**Patronising/bullying** *'Oh, go on – it won't take you long, you'll be away by half past.'*

Firmly restate the refusal, avoiding getting into a discussion about the length of time needed.

> *'Don, I can't – I have to be away on time today.'*

**Blaming** *'You're going to get me into trouble – if this isn't out today, I'll be for it.'*

Ignore this type of pressure and again restate the refusal.

> *'I wouldn't wish that, but I have to be away on time today.'.*

**Emotional blackmail** *'Don't forget, I helped you with those deliveries last month.'*

Again, ignore and restate the refusal.

> *'I know and I appreciated your help, but I have to be away on time today.'*

Make sure that you don't offer to ask a colleague on the person's behalf because you will still end up with the responsibility for getting it done.

**Keep it simple**

Don't give multiple reasons; you need to reinforce your argument, not dilute it. Reinforce it.

Don: *Can you help with this mailing? – I've got 3,000 to get out this evening.*

Suzanne: *I can't ... I've got to go this evening, I'm meeting Angie – I was at school with her – she's going into hospital tomorrow ... it's all a bit nasty. She was lovely to me when Barry left, so it's the least I can do.*

Give a reason if you want to, but then stick to it, using the broken record technique if you need to.

## Broken record technique

If you are faced with persistence, it is tempting to give different reasons for your refusal in the hope of adding weight to it:

Can you help with this mailing? I've got 3,000 to get out this evening.

I can't … I've got to go on time this evening.

Please, there's no one else who can do it.

But I've worked late three times this week.

Don't forget I helped you with those deliveries last month.

I know, but I'm seeing a friend this evening.

So make it a bit later.

I can't. She can only meet at 5.15 and she's going into hospital tomorrow.

There's no one else around.

I've so much of my own to do – I'm not going to get that done; so I can't take on any more.

But it will only be 30 minutes … I'll put them in envelopes. It's just the sorting out into areas; it won't take any time with both of us.

Well, I suppose I could do 15 minutes.

Instead, keep to the same reason, using the same words if you wish, or phrasing it in different ways, but essentially keeping the point.

Can you help with this mailing? I've got 3,000 to get out this evening.

I can't … I've got to go on time this evening.

Please, there's no one else who can do it.

I appreciate that, but I have to be away at five tonight.

Don't forget I helped you with those deliveries last month.

I know, but I can't stay late tonight.

There's no one else around.

I know, but I have to go on time this evening.

But it will only be 30 minutes … I'll put them in envelopes. It's just the sorting out into areas; it won't take any time with both of us.

Don, I have to be away at five, so I'm sorry, I can't help.

Oh … OK …

## Saying sorry

You might have noticed the word 'sorry' appearing in the example above. Make sure that you imagine it being said in a positive, closing tone, not an apologetic one! As explained in the last chapter, it is generally better to avoid the word, but if you can say it with a firm, closing tone, as above, it can add force to your point. You might wish to practise to ensure you can achieve the appropriate voice tone!

# 12 ... we've got a problem

Interpersonal problems are a fact of life. They should be minimised if you are maintaining a self-confident and assertive approach, but there is always the chance something will come up.

If, like most people, your tendency is to be passive, you are likely to ignore what is annoying you, not tackling it, but perhaps moaning about it to friends and colleagues. If it gets too much, you might snap – lose your temper and 'have it out' with the person, but a screaming row is not the best way to move things forwards.

## • First stage – try to nip it in the bud

Before doing anything, or saying anything to the person, just think through the situation calmly. Try to put yourself in the other person's shoes to get a perspective on how the situation looks to them.

- Describe the behaviour using specific, non-emotive words.
- Outline the effect of the behaviour on your feelings and subsequent words/actions.
- Try to see the situation from the other person's perspective.
- Plan changes to your non-verbal and verbal behaviour.

Read the example below before you try it for yourself.

(describe behaviour) *Ali, who used to do my job before me, regularly offers 'advice' on both work and personal issues. She does not wait to be asked and always prefaces it with phrases like "If I were you I'd ...".  She then keeps asking how I've got on with it (in other words have I done what she suggested?).*

(effect on you/words & actions)   *Resentment, feel that she is intruding, I feel undermined  in my work, I like time to think things through and not be cornered into* agreeing to do something I'm not sure of.

I tend to listen to her, knowing I will ignore her advice and am annoyed with myself for not saying something. I know some of the things she used to do were not successful and my manager is looking for me to change things.

(and from the other side) Ali did my job for seven years and achieved quite a promotion when she got her current job, so it is reasonable that she sees herself as 'expert'. She's older than me, and so has 'been there, done that' in almost every way (children, home, as well as work). I accept she means well and is trying to help me. She may feel a bit threatened that I might be seen to be doing a better job than she did.

(a strategy) I'll hear out her suggestion and then use phrases like "Thanks Ali, I'll bear that in mind when I decide", or "I'll try that if a backlog builds up". Particularly with domestic things, I'll try explaining that I need to think it through and decide for myself. I need to get her to see that I see her view as valid, but I want to make my own decisions.

I must appear generally comfortable and confident in what I'm doing and. when speaking to her. I need to retain good eye contact and a warm tone. I must reject her advice, not her as a person. If this does not work, will need to tackle her as a separate issue ... write a script.

Hopefully, a few comments like those above, combined with clearly displayed self-confidence in your ability to do the job Ali used to have, will sort out the problem.

Next time you have an interpersonal niggle, or a full-blown problem, give the approach a try:

The behaviour:

_____

_____

The effect on me:

_____

_____

_____

And how it might seem to the other person:

_____

_____

_____

My strategy (verbal and non-verbal, general appearance and specific to the person):

_____

_____

_____

_____

_____

## • And if that doesn't work – a direct approach

If you find that your strategy doesn't work – or is not as effective as you'd hoped – you might have to approach the person direct. Most people don't like conflict and find the idea of doing this very uncomfortable, so it's important to have a structured approach to what you plan to say.

You might wish to 'make an appointment' to see the person: ask them for a meeting, or for a few minutes of their time; or you might prefer to prepare what you want to say the next time they exhibit the behaviour which upsets you. Either way, try the approach below:

## Preparation

This is a return to the exercise above, to clarify the problem and its effects; also, to remind you of the other person's perspective.

At this stage, think about the timing, whether it's best to arrange a meeting or wait for the right moment. Think about who else will be around and whether that might be a problem for you, or cause unnecessary embarrassment.

## What to say: the 3i approach (introduce – impact – inform)

You are obviously immersed in the problem, but it is likely to come as a complete surprise to the other person. It is important that it is clear what you are talking about and that you say it in such a way that the other person does not become defensive.

So, you need to start by explaining what you're talking about and then its impact/effect on you. The third stage is to ask for the change you want. You may want to include an incentive: a general benefit of changing or something they will gain. This will be a flowing statement when you deliver it, but it is explained stage by stage below.

### Introduce

- Describe actions, not motives.
- Be specific and keep it simple.

  *'You've obviously got much more experience of this department, but when you offer advice based on how you did the job ...'*

### Impact (the effect on you)

- Keep calm and be specific.
- Take responsibility for your feelings ('I feel', not 'you make me feel').

  *'I feel undermined as I try to learn.'*

### Inform (of what you want)

- Be clear and realistic.

- Recognise their feelings.

- Offer negotiation.

> *'I appreciate that you're doing it to help me, but I'd prefer to try to work things out for myself, knowing I can come to you if I get stuck.'*

Don't plan to read this out (although the same structure does work well in writing). It is the basis for you to practise, so that you can say it clearly and calmly.

> *'You've obviously got much more experience of this department, but when you offer advice based on how you did the job, I feel undermined as I try to learn. I appreciate that you're doing it to help me, but I'd prefer to try to work things out for myself, knowing I can come to you if I get stuck.'*

If you need a structured approach, try the one below:

Introduce

_____

_____

Impact

_____

_____

Inform

_____

_____

_____

Incentive (if possible)

_____

_____

# 13 ... pleased to meet you

Many people find the actual moment of meeting someone uncomfortable, whether at work or socially, one-to-one or in a group. Often those worries centre on our fears about how others will see us, or the risk of making a fool of ourselves.   This causes a secondary problem: anticipating meeting people can become something to be worried about and we waste time and emotional energy dreading something that will probably turn out perfectly well.

## • Don't be selfish!

Before meeting someone new, whether one-to-one or at a party, it is easy to find things to worry about. Will they like me?  Will I understand what they're saying?  Will I say something stupid?  Am I dressed right?  With all this going on in your head, it's no wonder that you might feel stressed, but you're not the only one – other people are thinking the same thing.  Anyway, the person, or people, you are meeting are likely to be more interested in themselves than others.  People who are known for being great company are occasionally wonderful story-tellers or have a fascinating life – more commonly, they are great at asking questions and listening to the answers.  So don't worry about yourself, go into the situation being interested in the people you are to meet.

## • Meeting people one-to-one

Before you are to meet someone new, prepare yourself.  Try to find out their name in advance and something about them.  From this you can have a first question ready.

For example, if you are likely to meet the new finance director, Rosemary Carter, at a presentation tomorrow, you know:

*   her name
*   she's the finance director
*   she's new to the organisation
*   she's come from a retail background.

Remember, she knows nothing about you, so you have the upper hand! So when you're introduced, or if she smiles or greets you, you are ready to say 'Rosemary/Mrs Carter ... pleased to meet you – how are you settling in?' You can also have some follow-up questions ready, such as 'How have you found the move from retail?' Remember to listen to her answers and build on what she says to make a conversation – you're conversing, not interviewing her!

First of all, think about how you want to introduce yourself and practise saying it aloud.

> *'Hello, I'm Lucy Jones, the management accountant here.'*

> *'Hello, I'm Lucy Jones, Ellie's mother.'*

> *Hello, I'm Lucy Jones, Ellie's mother and the new girl on the PTA.'*

Next time you are to meet someone, do the preparation:

His/her name:

_____

Job/role/position:

_____

Why you're meeting:

_____

Two possible questions (about the person or situation):

_____

_____

Now practise aloud, so it sounds natural. It's very important to do this, rather than just reading the words silently!

## Casual meetings

Sometimes our initial meetings are much more casual; for example, collecting a visitor from reception, or an introduction to a fellow participant in a meeting. Practise greeting them confidently with a warm smile, the use of their name and probably a handshake. Always have a few general questions ready that will encourage easy chat for a few moments. For example, it doesn't help if you ask whether they managed to park (if they drove, they must have done or they wouldn't be standing there; if they didn't drive, it's a non-starter). Instead ask how their journey was. This can usually be developed into the route they took, difficulty in parking, vagaries of public transport, etc.

Prepare for casual meetings:

I'm likely to meet people casually if/when:

_____

_____

Two possible questions:

_____

_____

_____

Again, practise aloud.

## Meeting for the second time

When you meet someone again, greet them with warmth, using their name to show that it is the specific person you remember, not just meeting someone before: 'Hello Tom, nice to see you again." If possible, remember something about them or about an earlier conversation to refer to it: "How's the new car ... or not so new now, I suppose?"

## Remembering names

If you are introduced to a group of people, look at each one as you are introduced (try to say their name to yourself as you look). As early as you can in the conversation, use each person's name: 'I agree, Sarah, we've hardly seen any sun this year.' Or 'How long have your worked for the council, Kim?' You don't need to keep doing it, just one use will go a long way to fixing the names in your memory.

If you do find you've forgotten a name, just admit it and ask and again, repeat.

'I'm sorry, I've forgotten your name.'

'Liz McAvoy '

'Of course, <u>Liz</u> ... thanks.  So I'll ring with the web address tomorrow ...'

## • **Making conversation**

Of course, once you've got the initial meeting and greeting done, you are likely to need to sustain a conversation.

### Join in alongside, not opposite

Is the person you are to talk to lively and excited at the moment? Thoughtful and reflective? Morose and downbeat?  If you want to get a conversation going, align yourself to their mood at the start; you don't have to continue in that vein for long if you don't want to!

 'Isn't the weather awful? We've hardly seen the sun all summer.'

*'Oh I rather like it. My vegetables have been fabulous ... and all the tubs and hanging baskets look just perfect.'*

 'Isn't the weather awful? We've hardly seen the sun all summer.'

*'It has been exceptionally wet. I'm fed up with waking up to grey skies, but it has been good for the garden.'*

'I suppose so ...'

*'My vegetables have done well and tubs and hanging baskets look good.'*

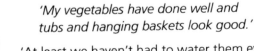 'At least we haven't had to water them every night.'

*'Have you been away at all?'*

## • Open the conversation

### Comment on something the person is wearing

Obviously it needs to be a positive comment! Make sure that you have some follow-up questions, such as where they bought it, if they have they had it for long, and if it was bought for a special occasion.

### Find out a little first

If you know that a new manager will be attending the meeting next week, find out where they've come from. You can then prepare a couple of questions to get the person talking.

> *'I hear you've come from the health trust – what changes are you finding in the private sector?'*

> *'What was it that attracted you to the private sector?'*

### Prepare some answers

You can never be sure what people will ask you, but some questions can reasonably be anticipated, particularly for social gatherings; things such as 'How do you know Gill?', 'What do you do?', 'Do you live around here?'

Whatever questions you anticipate, think of some information that you can add to the basic answer.

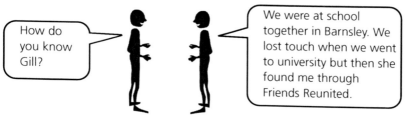

How do you know Gill?

We were at school together in Barnsley. We lost touch when we went to university but then she found me through Friends Reunited.

This gives the person the opportunity to develop conversation about growing up in Yorkshire, where you went to university, meeting up after many years, social networking websites, or to add a story of their own.

If you're asked what you do, don't just give a job title. Unless they're in the same field they are unlikely to be able to pick up on anything to develop the conversation. Add a little extra information to get things moving.

Of course, you need to be careful not to sound patronising by explaining the obvious.

'What do you do?'

'I'm an accountant … I spend my days looking at numbers.'

**Focus on the other person**

Once you've opened the conversation, keep it going by maintaining much of the focus on the other person. Really listen to what they're saying (rather than be planning what you are going to say next), and take your next question or comment from that.

Obviously you don't want to turn a conversation into an interview, or make the person feel they are being interrogated, but you'll usually find those who are deemed the best conversationalists simply ask open questions and let the other person talk.

**Don't top stories**

This is linked to the focus explained above. Awkwardness often makes us just add our experience to that of another and it can end up as an accidental competition to be the best.

'Have you been on holiday?'

'Yes, we went to Spain.'

'We were there last year … in fact we go most years.'

'We went to a golf resort. My husband has just discovered the game.'

*'We've played it for years – I started when I first met him and now the children have left home we play a couple of times a week.'*

This conversation runs the risk of grinding to a halt: the initiator missed two opportunities to develop it by asking about Spain (where they went, why they chose it, what it was like, would they recommend it), or about the husband playing golf (what made him choose it, how he's getting on, if the wife is tempted to play, the freedom/boredom of being a golf widow).

## • Practise and visualise

A lot of the situations above will require some practice. It is not necessary to learn a script; indeed, it would not sound right if you were to recite pre-prepared words. Practising aloud will help avoid words and phrases which are not necessary, and will help you become familiar with the words you want to say.

Stop and think what you want to say, and then turn away (from any notes you've written) and say it aloud as though you were in a real situation. Try and get the facial expression and body language to support it. Don't worry if you feel a bit foolish; most people would doing this alone in the front room, but you'll feel the benefit when you hear and see yourself appearing confident in reality.

Try to visualise yourself behaving confidently in the situation you find awkward. Try to find somewhere where you can relax without distractions and focus on picturing the situation. Use your eyes to see yourself walking tall, greeting people confidently, smiling as they speak, questioning to continue the conversation, and so on. Hear your voice tone, its warmth and interest as you speak, and feel the joy of knowing it's all going well.

# 14 ... in a meeting

## As a participant

For most people, meetings are a necessary evil and few like them, but it is important that you give your views and help move the group towards a decision.

Some meetings – usually team meetings, or those where you are comfortable with the people and knowledgeable about the subject – are easy. But a meeting with a group of strangers, or where you don't understand the points made by others, can be an awkward experience.

Remember that you have been invited because of your particular knowledge or experience and that is what people want you to contribute. If you are there representing the finance department, they are not looking for you to give the clinical perspective – they have the clinician there to do that. What they do want is the finance perspective, given in a way that is clear and respectful of the other positions around the table. No one will thank you if you sit, uncomprehending but silent. They will however respect you for having the confidence to say to the clinician, 'Excuse me, could you explain how that will affect your budget for next year?'

Read the points and questions below, then consider the case study before answering them.

- Identify a meeting where you'd like to change your behaviour.

- How do you tend to behave at the moment?

- What is it about the people, or situation, that causes you to behave this way?

- What do you need to change?

- Define a staged approach to implementing change.

*Alex is part of the graphic design team. He's been with the organisation for a year and is in line for promotion to senior designer some time in the next few months.  He considered the points and questions above and answered:*

- *Identify a meeting where you'd like to change your behaviour.*

  *The quarterly departmental budget meeting*

- *How do you tend to behave at the moment?*

  *I just keep quiet.*

- *What is it about the people, or situation, that causes you to behave this way?*

  *I don't really understand budgeting or accounts. I don't like figures and  was useless at maths at school.*

- *What do you need to change?*

  *I need to contribute – either to ask questions or when I see a problem looming – my budget on the last project was cut and I didn't say anything – that really caused problems.*

- *Define a staged approach to implementing change.*

  1. *Look up some of the jargon and technical terms they use.*

  2. *The next time someone uses a term I don't understand, I'll ask.*

  3. *I'll venture an opinion (must remember not to apologise for it).*

For any or each meeting you attend, identify your current behaviour and any changes you'd like to make.

- The meeting:

  _____

- Your current behaviour:

  _____

  _____

If you want to change that behaviour:

- What you tend to do at the moment:

  _____

- Why you do this:

  _____

  _____

- What needs to change:

  _____

  _____

How you can change:

- First step (something easy):

  _____

  _____

- Second step (a bit harder):

  _____

  _____

- Third step (when you can do this, you've cracked it):

  _____

  _____

You might prefer just to identify three actions you can take, rather than a staged approach.

To help develop your confidence with the group:

- Arrive a few minutes before the start, so you can get coffee and chat.
- Prepare yourself, so you know what each agenda item is about.
- Think through your views, so you can make points clearly.
- Demonstrate (non-verbally) that you are listening to others.
- Show your respect for the views of others – you don't persuade by putting people down.

- Lean forward slightly and keep your upper body 'open'.

- Keep your papers neatly stacked.

- Only apologise for mistakes, not for views stated or points raised.

- Speak clearly, calmly and try to avoid your voice's pitch rising – a lower voice has more authority.

## As the chairperson

Not many people consciously look to chair a meeting; more commonly it just comes with the job. It can be a daunting experience, and there are plenty of books to guide you through your role and responsibilities. From the perspective of 'Seeing me', the following might help:

Read the points and questions below, then consider the case study before answering them.

- Identify the meeting you're thinking of.

- How do you tend to chair it at the moment?

- What goes well?

- What/whom do you find difficult?

- How would you like it to be?

- Define a staged approach to implementing change.

> **Sheila** is the manager of the design team. She's an experienced designer, but was surprised to be promoted to the management role. Generally she enjoys her job, although she misses some of the hands-on work. She instigated a quarterly budget meeting to assess current projects against budget and to help prepare for new projects. She leads this meeting and considered the points and questions above.
>
> - Identify the meeting you're thinking of.
>
>   *Quarterly team meeting.*

- *How do you tend to chair it at the moment?*

  I try to keep to the agenda. I'm not sure what all the standard sections are for (e.g. matters arising).

- *What goes well?*

  I'm generally OK getting the quiet ones to contribute/ we usually finish about on time.

- *What/whom do you find difficult?*

  I have trouble stopping Jim taking over; I'm not comfortable if they argue. It's not really difficult to summarise as I go, but I sometimes forget to do so or to clarify the actions.

- *How would you like it to be?*

  I know it's not going to be sweetness and light, but I'd like it to be calm and supportive - and to achieve something.

- *Define a staged approach to implementing change.*

  1. I'm going to get a book and find out the purpose of all the sections - see what I'm supposed to do for each.

  2. I'm going to identify where actions are needed and mark them on my agenda. I'll talk to the minute-taker and ask her to remind me if I forget.

  3. I'm going to ask Jim specific questions and stop him as/before he gets off the point - I must acknowledge that I've taken his views on board though.

For any, or each, meeting you attend, identify your current behaviour and any changes you'd like to make.

- The meeting:

- How you chair at the moment:

  _____

  _____

If you want to change that behaviour:

- What goes well:

  _____

- What/whom you find difficult:

  _____

- How you'd like it to be:

  _____

How you can change:

- First step (something easy):

  _____

- Second step (a bit harder):

  _____

- Third step (when you can do this, you've cracked it):

  _____

You might prefer just to identify three actions you can take, rather than a staged approach

And in general:

- Liaise with the minute-taker, you will need to operate as a team.
- Arrive early and be ready to greet people (by name) and chat briefly.
- Start on time.
- Prepare well, so you know what you are doing at each stage of the meeting. For the main agenda items, know where decisions are needed.

- Manage the discussion towards a decision and ensure the decision is clearly stated.

- Remember they are looking to you to take control and won't thank you if the meeting drifts, achieves little and finishes late.

## As the minute-taker

In the office, there's usually a hierarchy from very senior, through layers of management, ending up with the person who usually takes the minutes.

In the meeting, there is one person chairing it, another minuting it and a range of people all invited because of their specific knowledge, experience or job. And that is the point: their knowledge is different. If one person knew it all, they could do the decision-making themselves.

It is easy to assume that other people know what you know. This breaks down into two parts: technical knowledge and general understanding.

### Technical knowledge

It would be hard to find a GP who would rationally expect their secretary to be able to diagnose the various ailments that crop up during the day, or understand the medical conditions. The problem comes when people just don't think – because they know something, it doesn't occur to them that someone else doesn't understand. On a mundane level, try asking any non-computer user to find the 'Windows' key – most will look for the word on a key; few will recognise the picture of a 'flag in the wind'.

### General understanding

Imagine asking a neighbour to buy you a pound of apples. You meant cooking apples (your family don't like eating them raw); your neighbour just assumed eating apples because that's a far more usual purchase for her. In meetings, people often assume others know what they're talking about, but it's often not the case. For example, the agenda item 'car park' will lead one person to assume it's about increasing the charges, another to assume it's about re-surfacing, another to assume it's about replacing the barrier, and so on. If you ask, it would be unusual to find someone who expects the minute-taker to know it all – they just assume.

The problem is that you are there to take the minutes and, if those minutes don't reflect the important information (particularly the actions), that whole discussion was wasted. So, keeping quiet if you don't understand, is really unhelpful and unprofessional.

Interrupting a meeting is a vitally important skill for a minute-taker. Those around the table will often have different memories of what went on (or may not be listening so have no memory of it at all).

For example, imagine that you didn't catch a budget that was agreed. You know who the main speaker was, so you ring the following day, only to find them admitting they were not sure, but suggesting you ring someone else. You ring that person, only to be given a figure you are sure is wrong, so you check with another participant – and are given a different figure. You could ring round all eight from the meeting and have eight different answers. If only you'd asked in the room, their misunderstanding would have been revealed and the matter cleared up. As it is, it will have to be on the next agenda.

Think of each participant standing on a plinth to show why they are there.

Your plinth says 'minute-taker'.

Make sure it is a plinth, not a hole.

You dig a hole by appearing to lack confidence through your non-verbal behaviour and by putting yourself down with phrases like:

I'm sorry, I missed who is doing that.

I haven't worked here long, so who is Sally?

Would you mind repeating those budgets? I couldn't keep up.

Most of the above won't be too much of a problem if it's said in a confident tone, but if not and it's combined with non-assertive body language, you will continually diminish the participants' view of your skills. So, you need to work on the non-verbal aspects and replace the statements above with more positive ones:

Excuse me, who is doing that?

Excuse me, for the minutes, what is Sally's surname?

Could you repeat those budgets for the minutes?

It is important to send a message: 'I'm here as minute-taker ... this is what I do ... and I do it well (you're working with a pro here!)'. Your role is important; if you were not there, one of the 'experts' would have to take the minutes. This would reduce the contribution of their expertise to the meeting, or reduce the information for the minutes. There is also a risk of bias and a lack of knowledge of the minute-taking process would probably result in lower quality minutes. You cannot expect them to respect you and your role if you do not show self-respect. If the self-confident message is received, they will treat you with more respect (not least because they'll see you as doing an important job) which, in turn, makes it easier to interrupt.

There are two aspects of confidence; the first is genuinely becoming more confident with the group. To help yourself:

- Arrive early and set the room up to look like a place to do business. Being there first, and so the one who greets the others, is good for your confidence.

- Offer the first person coffee and then pour your own and chat (prepare some things to chat about if you wish – see Chapter 13, 'Pleased to meet you'). Indicate the coffee to later arrivals and they can then join in the conversation.

- Try and remember small things about some individuals, such as new baby, change of job. Next time you can ask after the baby/job and start a conversation.

- Generally interact with them (eye contact, smile, nodding understanding).

- Make sure you have spoken to them before the meeting (to get agenda items, ask for background information, etc.), so you are at least a name and voice to them.

- Do as much of the admin as you can, and be seen to do it well.

- All the 'fake it' points below will also help your confidence.

  But – secondly – until you can make it, fake it! Try the techniques below to mask the fact that you are uncomfortable.

- Dress the part; if they are dressed casually, dress down; if they are in pinstripes, dress smartly.

- Don't draw attention to yourself if you are not comfortable with the attention (low necklines, skirts that ride up, clanky bangles on your writing hand).

- Take your papers in a ring-binder or similar, and use a smart pen.

- Think 'calm'. Don't dash about, move slowly and make sure your movements are controlled.

- Walk tall, shoulders down, head up.

- Smile in response to eye-contact, but don't grin into the middle distance!

- Sit back in your seat, straight-ish backed (don't bend over your notes like a child trying to stop someone copying).

- Preface interruptions with 'Excuse me', not 'I'm sorry'.

- Speak slowly and clearly – finish one word before you say the next.

### Interrupting

Not many minute-takers find interrupting easy. It does get better as you get more confident and as the group starts to be aware of your existence and role. To help yourself, and to be clear:

- Look at the person you are interrupting. Through your non-verbal behaviour, show that you want to speak next.

- Never say 'I'm sorry', although 'Excuse me' is fine.

- Ask for the information/explanation you require.

- Thank them and look down.

Read the points and questions below, then consider the case study before answering them.

- Identify the meeting you're thinking of.

- How do you tend to behave at the moment?

- What impression does that give of you?

- What would you like to change?
- Define a staged approach to implementing change.

*Amy is the PA to the Sales Director and has to take the minutes for the design department's quarterly budget meeting. It's a task she dislikes because the meeting is dominated by one strong character, it achieves little and she struggles to keep up with the mix of budget/finance discussion and the creative ideas that seem to be discussed for no obvious reason.*

- *Identify the meeting you're thinking of.*

  *Department budget meeting.*

- *How do you tend to behave at the moment?*

  *I keep a low profile, I sit near the front, but pull back from the table; I generally just look down at my pad and scribble.*

- *What impression does that give of you?*

  *I'm not sure they even notice me; I probably look very unwilling and rather disinterested.*

- *What would you like to change?*

  *I'd like them to appreciate the work I'm doing and I'd like to be confident in their company.*

- *Define a staged approach to implementing change.*

  1. *I'm going to work on looking the part (dress, body language, etc.).*

  2. *I'll then make sure I talk to them as they arrive – just chat.*

  3. *I must watch out for any action that isn't clear and I'll ask for clarification, deadline or whatever is needed.*

For any or each meeting you attend, identify your current behaviour and any changes you'd like to make.

- The meeting:

_____

- How you tend to behave at the moment:

_____

- The impression that gives:

_____

If you want to change that behaviour:

- you'd like it to be:

_____

How you can change:

- First step (something easy):

_____

- Second step (a bit harder):

_____

- Third step (when you can do this, you've cracked it):

_____

You might prefer just to identify three actions you can take, rather than a staged approach.

Remember – your role is very important. If you don't get the notes, they don't get an accurate record of the meeting and the reminder of their actions, and the whole thing is wasted.

# 15 ... give a presentation

Your presentation is prepared, you spent much of yesterday polishing it, and probably didn't sleep that well last night. Now, it's just a case of presenting yourself to your audience as a confident, interesting speaker.

Few people look forward to giving a presentation, but remember: most of the audience are interested in the content, not in you.

Ensuring that you are seen as the speaker you'd like to be has three aspects:

1. Preparing the presentation to the highest possible standard.

2. Your comfort in, and control over, the environment on the day.

3. The way you present yourself to your audience.

## Personal preparation

Apart from the obvious work in writing and timing your presentation, make sure that you observe the following three points.

### *Practise*

Go over your presentation aloud. Silent reading of your notes does not give you any feeling for how it sounds. When you first speak, it will sound unfamiliar. Find somewhere quiet and speak aloud, moving around the room picturing the audience there.

### *Practise your opening*

Although the whole presentation needs practice, put extra work into the opening. Plan how you will stand, where you will look, as well as what you will say. If you can get off to a good start, everything else is that bit easier.

### *Use your notes early*

Use notes, not a script, and prepare them early on so you are completely familiar with them as you practise. Write them on card, so they don't flop about. Cream or grey won't be as obvious as white. Always number them, so if they are dropped you can quickly sort them. Look at each note and speak that part of the presentation. Try and get to the stage where you can take the notes out of order and each one still reminds you of the point you want to make.

## Look the part

Wear clothes that you are comfortable in and that flatter your shape. Try and avoid anything that will draw unwelcome attention (for example, earrings that catch the light or an over-tight shirt). Your audience will have time to study you, so remember to polish your shoes and ensure every aspect of your appearance is suitable! Whilst in theory you should be judged on the quality of your presentation, the reality is that people do judge by appearances, so think of the person they want to see and try to match that expectation (in general, not necessarily down to every last detail). Remember that people might be 'looking up' to you on a stage; this might affect what you choose to wear.

## Know your environment

Get there early and familiarise yourself with the layout of the room. Make sure you know where the toilets are, when and where coffee will be served – people look on the presenter as someone of knowledge (on all things!) and will ask the strangest questions if they see you wearing a badge and recognise you as 'staff'.

## Check the equipment

### Laptop

Make sure it's plugged in and you know your presentation is loaded, which keys to hit, the level of the volume, etc. Where can you stand to reach it easily?

### Screen

Is it stable and at the right angle for clear display? Is it in the right place so you are not between the projector and screen?

### *Flipchart*

Is there enough paper? Pens? Is it the right height for you? Is it the correct side of you (on your left if you're right-handed)?

## While you're waiting

Once you are waiting to start, concentrate on looking calm and confident. Keep your head up, look warmly around, relax your body, lengthen your neck and hold your notes gently. Try to look as though you are looking forward to this (but beware looking smug). Be involved and interested in those around you.

## As you start

Don't apologise for anything, unless there's been a specific problem (for example, a delayed start). Avoid beginning with something like 'I was only told yesterday about this, so I hope you'll forgive ...'

Move to where you plan to stand, pause, look briefly at/over the audience with a smile and begin confidently, 'Good afternoon, I'm Tina Smith, the IT Manager, and I've been asked to give an overview of the new database we'll be using from January.'

## Keep going

As you move through your presentation, keep looking at the audience, but in a random way, not side-to-side as though watching a tennis match. Think of the letter M or W, and follow that shape approximately. No matter what their expressions, behave as though they were all rapt and interested – remember when someone is truly listening they often forget the social smile and frown in concentration.

Try to keep your body relaxed, your shoulders down and a warm expression on your face.

## Using the laptop

'Death by PowerPoint' is a commonly used phrase for a very good reason. It is an excellent program, very powerful, amazingly flexible and a vast improvement on boring OHP slides. However, it should not be used as an excuse to avoid giving the presentation.

### In moderation

Only use a slide where a visual image is better than words; for example, when comparing figures (chart or graph) or describing the layout of a site (map). It can also be used where you need to show a 'bigger picture' whilst explaining part of it; for example, to list six stages of a process, so the audience can see all six as each is explained. Do not then use different slides to explain each stage of the process – you might as well just e-mail them the slides.

### Headings only

Don't have paragraphs of text for your audience to read. Only a few will read them, and they will be ahead of you as speaker; the others will be looking into middle distance daydreaming, and some will simply be looking for typing mistakes.

### Don't look at your own slides

A glance to remind yourself is fine, but you are presenting to the audience, so always, always speak to them. Otherwise why not just e-mail them your slides to read with a coffee and biscuits?

### Proofread

Make sure that the text on your slides is grammatically correct, the punctuation is used properly, and they are consistent in colour, style, size and layout.

### Include blanks

Rather than leave a used slide on show, move to the next early or return to the desktop screen. Have some blanks ready, either in the appropriate colour or with an unobtrusive logo.

### Any questions?

Say at the start whether you want to be interrupted with questions, or that you'll take them at the end, or that there isn't time but that you're available afterwards or by phone/e-mail.

## And finally ...

Thank them for their time or interest as appropriate, smile and leave the 'stage'. It is best to stay around for personal questions or chat, rather than leave completely, and if others are speaking, make sure that you concentrate on them and what they have to say.

Now imagine a situation.

I'm likely to give a presentation on:

_____

My audience will be:

_____

How will they feel about the subject?

_____

What interests or worries them?

I tend to demonstrate my nerves by:

_____

_____

_____

The three things I want to remember to ensure I'm seen as confident:

1. _____

2. _____

3. _____

# 16 ... I'm the one for the job

Most people dread, fear and hate job interviews. But it is important to remember that they are the only way for potential employers to see how you and their organisation will match. They must think you have something or you wouldn't have been called. Most are not trying to catch you out, just find out more about what you know, what you can do and what you are like. Remember that the interviewer will be judged on the success of their hiring and may well be as nervous as you!

### What you know

These are your qualifications; they'll be listed on your CV and/or the job application, but you might find you are asked about them in a bit more detail or asked for your grades. Work-based qualifications should also be included here.

### What you can do

These are your skills, the application of your knowledge. These are not measured by examination and certificate, so you will need to demonstrate to the interviewer (not tell ... demonstrate) your competence.

### What you are like

This is your personality and your behaviour style, and it includes your self-confidence.

## Preparation

### Define the job you're being interviewed for

Read the job description and list the knowledge you need to have, the skills you need to demonstrate and the personality traits that make you ideal for the job. These are what you will need to emphasise during the interview.

Think about the knowledge you can prove in relation to the job. There is no point talking about your A grades in English and drama if you are applying for a job in the accounts department.

If you are currently applying for a job, list your relevant qualifications in order of importance to the job:

_____

_____

For each of the skills the job demands, select an example of when you have demonstrated that skill in a recent post.

Skills the job requires:    I've demonstrated this by:

_____    _____

_____    _____

_____    _____

_____    _____

_____    _____

Consider the type of person they are looking for and decide how you can demonstrate that you meet their criteria. For example, if you are applying for a post which involves meeting patients/relatives with a complaint about the hospital, you should come over as calm, sensitive, reassuring and with good reflective listening skills. It would not be appropriate to bounce into the interview with a beaming grin and tell amusing stories about your experience or last job.

They want someone who is:

_____

_____

**Find out some background on the organisation**

The Internet has made it easy to find out about any organisation, large or small. Prepare yourself by finding out some background and look in the press for news stories which may have an impact. At the very least, if the interviewer says, 'I suppose you'd like to know a bit about us,' you can respond with 'Well I know you provide cleaning materials within the NHS, but what are the main areas you specialise in?' or 'How has the current [health scare] affected your business?'

**Practise**

Consider the questions you are likely to face and practise your response. It is absolutely vital that you do this aloud, sitting in the sort of position you will be in during the interview. You might find it helps to face a mirror and address yourself. Make sure you look relaxed and don't fidget.

# The interview

### Appearance

The usual dress code for an interview is smart, but with so many organisations adopting smart/casual as their dress, it can be hard to define what smart is. If the job matters to you, try watching as staff come and go one morning or evening: do the men wear ties, are jeans commonplace? Generally, even in a less formal organisation, the more senior the job, the smarter the clothes and it is much better to err on the side of over-smart, rather than looking too casual.

Make sure that you can sit comfortably, and decently, in whatever you plan to wear and make sure your shoes and accessories all work together to create the image you want.

### Arrival and waiting

Always arrive on time, but take the phone number in case there is an unforeseeable delay. Calm yourself before you go in, so that your first impression is good to whoever is in reception.

## Greeting

When you are called in for the interview, take note of who has come for you: Is it your interviewer? His/her secretary? Remember the name, so you can use it again at the end of the interview, if not before. Make sure your right hand is free, so you are ready to shake hands, but do not force this if the other person does not offer. Be ready for small talk (journey, weather) on the way to the room, so that you have something to say.

Shake hands firmly, but without squeezing the hand. Make sure your handshake isn't limp, and don't wipe your hand afterwards.

## Send the right messages

Make sure that your non-verbal behaviour is sending the right messages:

### *Eye contact/expression*

- Look at the person you are talking to; try to relax your features, particularly tension around your eyes.

- Nod gently and slowly when listening to show your comprehension.

- Make sure your smile is appropriate – from a warm regard as a minimum, through to a broad smile at a humorous story.

### *Stance/movement/gestures*

- Stand and walk tall, with your shoulders back and down.

- Move positively and with energy, but don't rush or bounce.

- Don't 'hide' behind papers or a bag; relax your arms, so you carry items lower.

- Sit to the back of the chair and keep your back straight (but not ramrod!). Lean back to listen, but sometimes lean forward to emphasise a point.

- Keep your arms unfolded and show your palms occasionally as you gesture.

- Don't be afraid to move your arms to make a point, but beware overly expansive arm waving.
- If you're at a boardroom table, it's fine to put your hands or arms on the table, but don't do it on someone else's desk.

***Voice***

- Remember to breathe (before you speak and to punctuate your speech).
- Drop your voice tone to avoid the squeak that tends to come with nerves.
- Speak a little slower, try to finish each word before you say the next – it just paces you slightly.

## Answer the question

An interviewer might ask you to give your academic and work-based qualifications.   Don't recite a shopping list; detail a few, giving those that are most relevant to the job you are applying for and then group the others ("... and nine GCSEs).

As you are asked about your past experience and skills, keep the job you are applying for in mind.   Don't just tell someone what you are good at – demonstrate your skill through the examples you choose.   Try to show a range of skills through different examples, always with the emphasis on those which are relevant to the job.

### Difficult questions

An employer might notice something on your CV which may make you less suitable.   Be one step ahead by working out in advance where any shortfall may be and prepare yourself.   The interviewer is not necessarily trying to catch you out – they must have been interested enough to call you for interview.

'I see you haven't worked with computers for a few years.'

*'No, it's one of the reasons I'm interested in this job – I enjoy computer work and would like to get back into it and bring my skills back up to speed.'*

## The trickier questions

### *Tell me a bit about yourself as a person*

The interviewer doesn't want to know the names of your siblings and breed of your dog. Plan three or four points which will show you in a good light in relation to the job. For example, team sports if the job involves team work, a fitness hobby if there are physical demands, etc. Practise saying it aloud, so that it comes naturally.

### *What are your strengths?*

Again, identify what the job requires and tailor your answer accordingly, choosing the two or three most relevant. As with your skills, find brief examples to illustrate them.

### *And your weaknesses?*

This is much trickier. Again, the trick is to find what's important for the job. For example, in a role where checking figures is important, you might say you have a tendency to be over-careful in proofreading and fear it sometimes might take too long (but you feel it's important to get it right first time).

### *What's your greatest achievement?*

This doesn't have to be something spectacular. The medal you got for completing a five-mile walk for charity is just as much an achievement for you as the medal won by a top athlete at an international event is for that athlete. Maybe you've overcome a major setback or disability? Done anything outside your comfort zone? Don't apologise for how small your achievement is, just explain why you are proud of it; for example:

> *'I completed an eight-mile walk for Cystic Fibrosis earlier this year. I hadn't done any exercise for years, but was surprised by how unfit I was when I started. I trained for a month and completed it quite easily. I'm doing a lot more exercise now.'*

## Where do you see yourself in five years' time?

You will need to gauge whether the organisation wants people who will stay in the same role for years or whether they look to develop and promote staff. Most would hope that you will still work there in five years' time, but beware appearing to want your would-be manager's job within months. For example:

> *'I would see myself within [organisation], hopefully having developed my skills and built on my experience and doing more work in the sales environment.'*

**Ali** *has applied for a job as manager of the reception/switchboard team. She has put a lot of work into her CV and application form, and has identified the knowledge, skills and personal attributes the job requires and ways to demonstrate that she is a suitable candidate. She has been shortlisted for two similar jobs but not been appointed, and she's aware that she was unprepared for questions such as 'what is your greatest achievement?'.*

*Two nights before the interview, Ali has the house to herself, so she pours herself a glass of wine, finds some inspiring music and sets to work – the result is as follows:*

Tell me a bit about yourself.

*'I've worked in a variety of roles, mostly customer-focused areas. I started as a receptionist in the city hospital and have worked my way up through a variety of administrative jobs and, having covered the team manager's job for maternity, I now feel ready to take on a management role.'*

What do you consider your strengths?

*'I'm well-organised and self-disciplined. I'm friendly and genuinely interested in people. My experience of helping my disabled aunt has given me some useful insights in seeing things from another perspective.'*

Are there any areas where you feel you need to develop?

*'I can get a bit too involved in people's problems and wanting to help them navigate the system. I recognise I will have to be careful of this in a management role.'*

What have you done that you are particularly proud of?

*'I organised and led a team of neighbours to renovate our village hall. We got £40,000 in grants from different places and used contacts, villagers' skills and so on to save money. It's now a thriving village centre.'*

Where do you see yourself a few years from now?

*'Still within [organisation], I would hope to be looking to develop into a broader management role, perhaps within a service unit.'*

P.S. Ali didn't get that job, but she got the next one she applied for!

# 17 Time for me

*Think of yourself as a rechargeable battery ...*
*you need your charge 'topped up' frequently ...*
*... but also need a periodic complete recharge if you are going to keep*
*maximum power!*

The full recharge of your battery is an annual holiday, a week or two away from it all, from which you return refreshed and ready to go ... until your battery begins to wear down again. Even a short break or day out can bring great benefits to your mental and physical state.

If you don't look after yourself, who will? If you are to cope with a pressured lifestyle, you also need to build in some top-up charges which can make the difference between keeping going and going under. These tend to get forgotten and we keep going, discharging our battery and working on; like the toy train left running around the track while its owner has gone on to play with something else.

So what are these top-ups? Just as holidays can be divided into the longer annual holiday and other short breaks, top-ups can be divided into the once or twice-a-week hour or two out (such as a walk with friends, or a yoga class), and shorter two- to 20-minute breaks in a day. If holidays are made up of days away, these are holiminutes!

## • Take a holiminute!

Try to build in a short period of 'me time' in each day – do something you want to do. You might read the paper, watch your favourite programme, or just sit still. Don't feel guilty, you will increase your effectiveness after a short recharge.

Think about the holiminutes that five members of the finance department take:

Tom stops the car at a local beauty spot and just stands and looks at the view for five minutes.

Sara curls up on the sofa and reads her book.

Sascha drives a longer route home, via a country road which is easier to drive than the roundabouts, traffic jams and frustrations of the quicker more direct route.

Pearl has a 20-minute sleep when she gets home at 2.30 before collecting her children.

Mark goes out for a run.

Your fairy godmother has given you a bonus hour, once a week, on the condition that you use it on yourself. What would be your top three uses of that time?

1. _____

2. _____

3. _____

Do your choices have anything in common? (Are they to do with getting outside? Seeing friends? A hobby?)

Think whether you would benefit from a regular hour out, for example a book club or exercise class. Or would you prefer a different activity each week – a walk one weekend, a mid-week drink with friends, an hour on the sofa with a magazine?

Identify one thing you would like to do as a holiminute:

1. What time of day is the most likely to be suitable?

   _____

2. What day/s of the week?

   _____

3. What is the next step to take to ensure you get that holiminute?

   _____

Now sort it!

Don't forget ... you can also take a holisecond! Try to stop for just a few seconds to admire the view, enjoy the blue sky, listen to the sound of children playing, feel the warmth of winter sun on your face.

Remind yourself of two or three things, like those above, that make you feel good:

_____

_____

Now take the opportunities as they come to enjoy your holiseconds.

### Try this

For two – three weeks, pause each evening and ask yourself what has made you happy during the day (large or small events, even fleeting moments). Make a note to remind yourself of these and, at the end of that time, consider what you can draw from your answers. How can you actively build happy moments into your day?

Don't feel guilty ... Remember that toy train. When its batteries are flat, it's motionless and spent; the child will be very disappointed!

# 18 Face forward, look up!

Now that you've worked through the book, filling in the sections and working on small personal action plans, have a look at a more general picture. Consider the questions below, take the steps you need to and then review your progress. Return to this every few months, or whenever you need to.

1. Where are you 'at' at this time?

   _____

2. What's good?

   _____

3. What would you like to change?

   _____

4. Why do you want to change?

   _____

5. What steps can you take to prepare for change?

   _____

6. How can you implement change?

   _____

   _____

   _____

   _____

7. How will you know when you have achieved success?

   _____

8. Review: What did you do right? With hindsight, is there anything you should have done differently?

   _____

   _____

Joanna Gutmann is a trainer, specialising in administrative skills. Originally a secretary, her work with support staff in a range of organisations has given her an insight into the strains and pressures of today's working environment where people often feel they are not seen, let alone taken into account. This book aims to provide practical guidance in building self-confidence and assertive communication, and support in developing the skill of presenting a competent and confident image to the world.

Lightning Source UK Ltd.
Milton Keynes UK
19 February 2011

167763UK00001B/14/P